THE VALIDITY OF PSYCHO-ANALYSIS

J. G. STARKE

The Validity of Psycho-Analysis

Angus and Robertson · Publishers

First published in 1973 by

ANGUS AND ROBERTSON (PUBLISHERS) PTY LTD

102 Glover Street, Cremorne, Sydney
2 Fisher Street, London
107 Elizabeth Street, Melbourne
167 Queen Street, Brisbane
89 Anson Road, Singapore

National Library of Australia
Card number and ISBN
hard bound edition 0 207 12610 0
paper bound edition 0 207 12611 9

Registered in Australia for transmission by post as a book
PRINTED IN AUSTRALIA BY HOGBIN, POOLE (PRINTERS) PTY. LTD, SYDNEY

TO FRANCES

The mind is its own place, and in itself
Can make a Heaven of Hell, a Hell of Heaven

John Milton, *Paradise Lost,* Book I, 254-55

PREFACE

This book contains an evaluation by a lawyer of the basic principles and concepts of psycho-analysis; of its status as an established science of the human personality; and of its contribution to thought in general.

At the same time the book serves as an up-to-date introduction to psycho-analytical doctrine, that may be found useful by lawyers, social workers, marriage guidance counsellors, and students of sociology, political science, and international relations. The main theoretical and practical aspects of the subject are treated. Moreover, the two appendices may prove helpful to readers approaching the subject for the first time: Appendix I contains a short history of the development of psycho-analysis, covering the outstanding features only; Appendix II provides a glossary of the principal psycho-analytical terms.

In addition, Appendix III contains a revised version of an earlier article by the author on modern developments in psychiatry and the law. This supplements Chapter XIII.

The author has been engaged in research for a number of years in, and has published studies on the relationship of psycho-analytical theory to law and international relations.[1] He was encouraged to write the present book by the increasing attention which lawyers and law teachers have been giving to the subject of psycho-analysis. Among a number of valuable contributions, there have been Professor Albert A. Ehrenzweig's book on psycho-analytic jurisprudence, published in 1971, and his article 'A Psycho-Analysis of the Insanity Plea' in the January 1964 issue of the *Yale Law Journal* (pp. 425-441); Professor Joseph Goldstein's study of 'Psycho-Analysis and Jurisprudence' in the *Yale Law Journal,* May 1968 (pp. 1053-1077); and A. Katz, 'A Psycho-Analytic Peek at Con-

1 'Modern Developments in Psychiatry and the Law', *Australian Law Journal,* Vol. 16 (1942), pp. 227 *et seq.*; *Introduction to the Science of Peace* (*Irenology*), Leyden 1968; and 'The Treatment of Insanity' (1951), paper presented to the Medico-Legal Society of New South Wales.

spiracy', *Buffalo Law Review,* Vol. 20 (1970), pp. 239-251. Apart from this, psycho-analysis has for some time now been receiving attention in certain major law schools, in particular the Harvard Law School, the Yale Law School, and the Law School of the University of California. The Harvard Law School currently provides a course under the title, 'Psycho-Analytic Theory and Legal Assumptions', designed to familiarize students with psycho-analysis as a systematic theory of human behaviour, and to explore its relevance to a variety of legal issues.

It may not be over-prescient to envisage a future time when such a course as that in the Harvard Law School will be provided by the majority of leading law schools, and when a knowledge of the basic principles and terminology of psycho-analysis is considered to be a necessary part of the standard intellectual equipment of practising lawyers, and of workers in the social sciences generally.

J. G. STARKE

CONTENTS

Chapter I

PSYCHO-ANALYSIS—A CULT OR A SCIENCE?

Psycho-Analysis is a term not free from ambiguity, and unfortunately it has been given wide meanings, based on misconceptions and misapprehensions. As used in this book, it denotes a composite of the following: (a) a special procedure for the investigation of unconscious mental processes and forces; (b) a therapeutic technique, based on such investigation, for the treatment of neurotic or emotional disorders; and (c) a body of knowledge and doctrine obtained and developed from, and on the basis of this procedure of investigation, and of this therapeutic technique.[1] The qualification is that this collective discipline was founded by Professor Sigmund Freud (1856-1939) and has continued to be moulded, more or less, along the the lines laid down by him during his lifetime. Although he was able to establish the foundations of psycho-analysis, with the aid of collaborators, Freud could not dictate future development and the introduction of new refinements. He appreciated that this was a task best left to posterity.

This book is not at all concerned with schools of theory or practice of a non-Freudian character. Rather, it is confined to psycho-analysis as that term is understood by the principal organized bodies in the field of Freudian psycho-analysis, such as the International Psycho-Analytical Association, the British Psycho-Analytical Society, and the American Psycho-analytic Association.

1 This three-fold meaning of psycho-analysis is widely recognized, in particular by psycho-analysts themselves. (See, e.g., H. Flournoy, *La Psychanalyse, les Médecins et le Public,* Geneva 1924, p. 3, and Heinz Hartmann, in Sidney Hook (ed.), *Psychoanalysis, Scientific Method and Philosophy,* New York 1959, p. 4.)

There have been various criticisms of psycho-analysis, some of which are considered in later chapters. Indeed no discipline in the whole history of human thought has been subjected to such a degree of censorious comment.

One of the principal forms of attack has been that psycho-analysis is not a 'true' science, but a cult, such as, for example, the cults of nudism and of vegetarianism. To deal with this criticism objectively it is necessary to clarify the meanings of 'cult' and of 'science'. We shall first discuss the nature of a cult.

Nature of a cult

A cult, in the sense of that term as used by the critics of psycho-analysis, denotes both a body of practices and a system of beliefs, subscribed to by a number of persons in the faith that certain benefits to themselves and/or others will accrue if the practices and beliefs are undeviatingly followed, irrespective of whether or not these are scientifically established to be valid.[2] So it is that some cults, for example that of nudism, may profess to be based upon scientific proof that adherents will reap definite advantages. Other cults, particularly religious or neo-religious cults, may be purely a matter of dogma, often associated with a superstitious fear of punishment by occult forces for any deviations.

In certain cults, if not in all, there is the implication that the advantages sought to be obtained will accrue solely and exclusively from the practice of the particular cult, and cannot come about in any other way. An example is the cult of playing-field sports followed by many English schools, and which is justified on the basis that only by engaging in these sports will boys be able to cultivate the virtues of manliness, discipline, and ability to accept or overcome failures in their future careers.

It is further characteristic of some cults that they involve, as essential components, a number of ritual-like practices, on the one hand, and sacerdotal, often quasi-taboo restraints and abstentions on the other.

As the term 'cult' is used currently, it is fair to say that many cults are oriented to values of a serious nature and are far from discreditable. This is noted to preclude suggestions that some critics who treat psycho-analysis as a cult are necessarily saying that its aims and basic functions are unworthy.

[2] The term 'cult' may also be employed to signify a sect, meaning a group of persons, in a minority, devoted to a special creed or set of values.

Nature of a science

The acknowledged general characteristics of a science may be defined by reference to the fundamentals of all scientific inquiries: the prosecution of studies and research directed to the ascertainment of truths and realities; the evaluation of data-material without preconceived judgment; and some form of unity and systematization resulting in the enunciation of a more or less coherent body of laws, norms, principles, theories, generalizations, and categories.[3] A basic assumption of every scientific discipline is that the empirical facts examined will enable the drawing of inferences above and beyond the subject-matter.

In this connection, there are some fallacies which require to be exposed. In no science is it possible to achieve finality in the inferences drawn, or in the predictions resting on such inferences. Scientific laws are not invariably formulated with absolute definitiveness. Indeed, as a science develops, and with the accumulation of additional relevant information, it may represent a process of refinement of approximations, and, in some areas, may scarcely progress beyond pure approximations.

A science may be composed of generalizations expressing probabilities, or in the form of statements of tendencies, and may include, on an even lower level, formulations of reasonable expectations. Moreover, every science works with the aid of the *hypothetico-deductive* technique, involving the hypothetical postulation of statements of laws and theories, the verification and validation of these and the confirmation, rejection or modification of the hypothetical statements upon proof of their validity or fallibility.

Several other misconceptions of the nature of a science, which bear on the question whether psycho-analysis is a scientific discipline, need also to be dispelled. One lingering misapprehension is that a discipline which is not founded on data obtained from 'normal' methods of research cannot be truly scientific. 'Normal' methods of research apparently refer to laboratory and statistical techniques, so that data available from private experience and observation would, presumably, not qualify. It is, however, erroneous to treat the origin of the data examined as the criterion

[3] For emphasis on these essential characteristics of unity and systematisation as marking a science, see Leonard Nelson's *Socratic Method and Critical Philosophy*, New Haven 1949, and *System of Ethics*, New Haven 1956. Both are translated from German.

of a science, the hallmark of which is, rather, the application of the hypothetico-deductive method to empirical material, irrespective of its source. If the progress of a discipline can result in the derivation of hypotheses that can be empirically tested, that is sufficient, generally speaking, to entitle that discipline to the appellation of a science.

A second misconception lies in the belief that observable phenomena are susceptible of only one explanation in terms of a physical nature, to the exclusion of any generalization embodying some intangible theoretical concept. This would negate the scientific character of important areas of mathematics and physics, in which intangible theoretical concepts play so important a role. There is also the consideration that observable phenomena may have to be considered in different frames of reference, so that different generalizations may be necessary.

A third error is to regard a postulated law as unscientific because it may embrace unobserved, as well as observed data. If such a view were correct, some of the most fundamental laws of physics would never have been propounded in the first instance, because they involved a prediction of a provisional character regarding unobserved or hitherto unobservable phenomena. Perhaps an apt illustration in that connection is Einstein's general theory of relativity, in its application to the working of gravitation.

Some special points regarding the nature of a science are non-controversial, and cannot be challenged. There is the point, to begin with, that scientific laws and generalizations are open to continued review, modification, and amplification. This is illustrated sufficiently by the history of modern physics. A theory does not cease to be scientific because it is formulated in a provisional manner, subject to revision and extension in the light of additional experience. Nor again does a science shed its scientific character because those who profess it may have acute differences of opinion in respect to laws and theories propounded. So, in the science of physiology there are, currently, widely divergent approaches among physiologists towards, for example, the functions of the central nervous system, and the precise nature of certain physico-chemical aspects of the human body.

Lastly, it is not a necessary characteristic of a science that its teachings ensure absolute certainty in the prediction of future behaviour. Otherwise, having regard to the fallibility of predictions by, say, weather bureaux, meteorology would scarcely merit the appellation of a science.

Arguments that psycho-analysis is a cult

Those who argue that psycho-analysis is a cult take their stand on the fact that professional psycho-analysts have, generally speaking, remained undeviatingly loyal to the basic principles established by Freud and his collaborators, and do not apply or favour the divergent theories of non-Freudian schools of analytical and depth psychology. A cogent answer to this argument is that it rests upon an extremely narrow view of the range of application, and of the influence of psycho-analysis. A great number of psychiatrists and psychologists, who are not professional psycho-analysts, are nevertheless using the classical methods of psycho-analysis as their current tools of trade and consciously adhering to psycho-analytical principles which they have found to be effective in practice. It is also fairly claimed that sociologists, anthropologists, and social workers throughout the world are pursuing their labours more efficiently through the insights provided by psycho-analysis. The social and behavioural sciences generally would scarcely be the same without the keys to the understanding of social phenomena and individual conduct provided by psycho-analysis. This can be seen at a glance by reference to *A Dictionary of the Social Sciences* (editors, Gould and Kolb, 1964), compiled under the auspices of UNESCO and which defines certain major psycho-analytical concepts. It is significant also that numerous philosophers have not treated psycho-analysis as a cult, but have considered it upon its merits as a discipline, seeking to provide explanations of some aspects of human personality and of the behaviour of groups.[4]

Some opponents of psycho-analysis have made much of two allegedly cult-like features of its application in therapeutic practice. One is the use of the couch on which patients must lie during treatment, for the purpose of expressing their thoughts, in free association, so that nothing which comes into the mind is held back. It is maintained that the couch has become a ritualistic component of psycho-analytical therapy. The other supposed cult-like feature is the rule, which used to be fairly rigidly adhered to, that it was not generally for a psycho-analyst to give advice to a patient on how to cope with concrete problems of his personal life, such as his

[4] For the opinion, however, that there is lack of genuine communication between psycho-analysts and philosophers, the former being unfamiliar with the philosophy of science, the latter disregarding the mass of empirical detail upon which psycho-analysis is based, see John Hospers, 'Philosophy and Psychoanalysis', in Sidney Hook (ed.), *Psycho-analysis . . .* , p. 336.

career, marital relations, and matters of finance, notwithstanding that these may have contributed to the intensification of his neurotic or emotional disorders. With regard to the couch, the justifications for its use appear rational rather than ritualistic; namely that it is a pragmatic means for ensuring that a patient is in the most relaxed position, without being disturbed by seeing the face of the psycho-analyst and drawing conclusions. At the same time, it seems an insistence upon the couch for all patients can be too pedantic; some become too drowsy and cannot think in a horizontal position, or are constitutionally unable to talk to four blank walls, or may have their guilt and inferiority feelings accentuated by being made to lie prostrate before an unseen physician.[5]

As to the non-advice rule, that also was based on rational rather than ritualistic grounds: to enable the patient to come to his own considered decisions after proper insight into the reasons for his condition. This rule could be carried too far and has now tended to be relaxed. If, for example, a patient lacks the will to recover, because he is following the wrong career, or because he needs legal advice in regard to his marital relations, it may be wrong not to suggest obvious conclusions. In this, it should be for a psycho-analyst to maintain a proper balance between the need for patients to make their own decisions and the exigencies of their outside life.

To sum up, professional psycho-analysts can be exonerated from the charge that they have turned psycho-analysis into a cult. It is difficult to see how such a charge could be fairly made against Freud, and his collaborators during his lifetime.

Having said this, one must nevertheless point out that there are dangers of a cult of psycho-analysis developing, not among professional psycho-analysts, but among non-professional members of the public who may make wild claims for psycho-analysis as a cure-all for the whole range of mental disorders, and as a complete explanation for all aspects of the human psyche. Yet this would be no different from a cure-all cult developing in respect to any other aspect of medical therapy; for example, a cult as to the taking of vitamin tablets as an all purpose remedy.

Psycho-analysis as a science

Almost from the outset, and until the end of his life, Freud, who had an early scientific training in neurophysiology and who was to

[5] There is certainly more flexibility at the present time than in the early days of psycho-analysis, with less rigid insistence that patients must lie down, instead of sitting up if they so wish.

uphold continually the thesis that the aim of scientific thought was to achieve correspondence with external reality, applied the hypothetico-deductive method in the progressive development of psycho-analytic doctrine.[6] He postulated hypotheses on the basis of observational data, empirically testing and assessing his hypothetical theories against fresh data and undeniable inferences, and continually revised, modified, and reformulated his views after such testing and assessment.[7] This process was pursued in the most objective manner, with the aid of collaborators who approached the subject similarly. Concepts, hypotheses, and laws or theories were not derived until justified by the data observed. It is a mark of this deliberately pursued scientific process of investigation that time and again Freud would rhetorically raise questions that he found himself unable to answer to his satisfaction, and would also indulge in speculations, as distinct from theories, in regard to points which he considered were baffling.[8]

It is certainly not a valid criticism, as we have already seen, that the data available to Freud came mainly from observation of patients in consulting rooms and hospitals, and also from the material obtained by anthropologists, instead of emanating from scientific laboratories and detailed statistical studies. Moreover, a distinguished psycho-analyst has pointed out that each single clinical case represents, for purposes of research, 'hundreds of data of observed regularities, and in hundreds of respects', so that it is fallacious to discount the scientific value of observational data from this source.[9]

[6] Indeed it should not be overlooked that, in measure as they crystallized, each of Freud's theories represented the end-result of a long and gradual development in his scientific thought on the subject. His struggles and gropings, as a scientist, in order to reach the truth, or to propound some tentative law or theory, are mirrored not only in his published studies and books, but also in his private correspondence. See, e.g., the correspondence with Dr Wilhelm Fliess reproduced in M. Bonaparte, A. Freud, and E. Kris (eds), *Origins of Psycho-Analysis,* London 1954.

[7] For a general treatment of Freud's scientific approach, see Meissner, 'Freud's Methodology', *Journal of American Psychoanalytic Association,* Vol. 19 (1971), pp. 265-309.

[8] As Dr Heinz Hartmann pointed out, Freud did not speak of psychoanalysis as a 'system', but rather stressed its incomplete character, its flexibility, and the tentative nature of much of it, with the repeated necessity for adjustments and reformulations of various aspects of theory. See Sidney Hook (ed.), *Psychoanalysis* . . . , p. 4.

[9] Dr Heinz Hartmann, 'Psychoanalysis as a Scientific Theory', in Sidney Hook (ed.), *Psychoanalysis* . . . , p. 21 n. On the other hand, the scientific limitations of clinical case studies have been stressed by other

The use of the hypothetico-deductive method by the psycho-analytic movement did not cease with the death of Freud but has continued to this day. This may be seen in the contributions to psycho-analytic literature and doctrine by members of the International Psycho-Analytical Association. The scientific approach of psycho-analysts generally is also reflected in their feeling that psycho-analysis is still far from being a closed system, and that a higher degree of systematization is needed in order to improve its standing as a scientific discipline.[10] The necessity for a more refined methodology has been a constant preoccupation. Scientific method governs even the conduct of an individual therapy, itself a form of scientific investigation of personality problems. As Professor Arlow has said:

> It should be acknowledged that psychoanalysis is not an esoteric cult in which the analyst foists upon gullible patients a preconceived mumbo-jumbo inherited from Freud. Psychoanalytic therapy is a meticulously painstaking investigation into human mental processes. It is by no means a perfect experimental tool, but it is, nevertheless, a rational and objective procedure, governed by strict methodological considerations and operating within accepted canons of the scientific method.[11]

Perhaps one of the most cogent facts proving the scientific character of psycho-analysis is the extent to which a number of psycho-analytical concepts have been adopted, almost without question, by modern psychiatry. Among these are concepts such as identification, displacement, sublimation, repression, projection, compensation, reaction formation, fixation, defence mechanism, and regression. In legal practice, it is rather striking, if not humorous, to find non-analytical psychiatrists in the witness-box, who on the one hand ridicule psycho-analysis, and on the other hand, somewhat inconsistently, employ these concepts for the purpose of their testimony.

Much criticism has been directed at psycho-analysis because of its postulation of the unconscious, of a tripartite division of the mind

writers, and it has been said that more formalized and more systematized studies of the therapeutic process of psycho-analysis ought to be conducted; see R. S. Wallerstein and H. Sampson, 'Issues in Research in the Psychoanalytic Process', *International Journal of Psycho-analysis,* Vol. 52 (1971), pp. 11-47.

10 Dr Hartmann, ibid., pp. 4-5. See also Charles Brenner, 'Psychoanalysis and Science', *Journal of American Psychoanalytic Association,* Vol. 16 (1968), pp. 675-96.

11 In Sidney Hook (ed.), *Psychoanalysis . . .* , p. 211.

into the ego, the id and the super-ego, and of a death instinct. With regard to the unconscious, it is claimed that such a concept is unscientific, partly because unconscious forces and processes are unobservable,[12] and partly because it is thought that at some time in the future a more exact theory may be formulated in terms of physico-chemical activities in the central nervous system. Both these grounds are unacceptable. The unconscious is a theoretical concept like other abstract and invisible concepts employed in the sciences to explain the working of tangible, concrete phenomena. It serves the purpose of making certain predictions, and of enabling inferences to be otherwise drawn. Nor does the concept of the unconscious exclude an explanation in terms of physico-chemical processes operating in the brain, any more than such a physico-chemical explanation ought to exclude the theory of the unconscious. There can be alternative explanations, or explanations in different frames of reference, without these necessarily being unscientific. The ego, the id, and the super-ego are similarly higher-level theoretical concepts, which are scientifically valid, irrespective of their abstraction and intangibility, and irrespective also of the fact that in the future an alternative theory of explanation may be found in terms of physico-chemical processes in the central nervous system.

These considerations apply also to Freud's postulation of a death instinct, but here an additional point arises. It is maintained that the theory of a death instinct is unscientific because there can be no satisfactory explanation of why there should be such a destructive instinct present in man, one which according to Freud, 'functions in every living being, striving to work its ruin and reduce life to its primal state of inert matter'.[13] If such an argument were correct, then a generalization of science which was descriptive only, and stopped short of being explanatory, could not be scientific. This would negate the scientific character of some of the most fundamental theories of modern physics.

It is true that in a number of respects psycho-analysis is an incomplete discipline. Much remains to be done and explained, and much has to be related to new developments in neurology. Also there is controversy among psycho-analysts in regard to

12 Yet it is hardly possible to deny the weight of evidence proving that people may have motives of which they are not consciously aware. See John Hospers, in Sidney Hook (ed.) *Psychoanalysis . . .* , p. 337.

13 Exchange of Open Letters, Albert Einstein-Sigmund Freud, published by International Institute of Intellectual Co-operation, League of Nations 1933, p. 45.

numerous matters, some important and some of a minor character. Nor does psycho-analysis ensure absolute certainty of success in the treatment of those nervous or emotional disorders for which, as a method of therapy, it is best suited. Yet a science which stumbles here and there, and which is still in process of development, is no less a science on that account. For these reasons, the true nature of psycho-analysis as a science ought not to be denied.

Chapter II

THE CONCEPT OF THE UNCONSCIOUS

The division of the human psyche into the conscious and the unconscious is a fundamental postulate of psycho-analysis, both central in its theoretical structure and basic in therapy. One of the most widespread misconceptions of psycho-analysis, nourished by the natural feeling of men and women that they have dominion over their own minds, is that psycho-analysts accord absolute primacy to the unconscious, treating the conscious part of the psyche as purely of secondary importance. This is not correct. The question is not at all one of the relative importance of the conscious and unconscious divisions of the mind, but rather of the special role which each has to play, both by itself and in relation to the other. Nor can it be said that psycho-analysis insists on always drawing, and for all purposes, a sharp distinction between the two divisions.

Another aspect of this misconception is that psycho-analysis has been interpreted as making a deliberate attack on rationality. Nothing could be further from the truth. Both in theory and therapy, psycho-analysts give proper weight to the operation of conscious human reason and intelligence, for the purpose of coping with the demands of the unconscious. Indeed, to the extent that they are visionaries, most psycho-analysts look to a future time when, as the conscious minds of men become more mature at the rational level, mankind will be less impelled by unconscious forces.[1]

1 This is reflected in the much quoted statement by Freud that 'in the long run, nothing can withstand reason and experience'. See *The Future of an Illusion,* in the *Complete Psychological Works of S. Freud,* Vol. XXI, p. 54.

It is sometimes stated that since the death of Freud, in 1939, the importance of the unconscious as a basic premise of psycho-analysis has waned. This also is untrue. What is meant by the statement, perhaps, is that there is a current trend among many psycho-analysts concerned with therapy to give more attention than formerly to the character or constitution of persons undergoing psycho-analysis, and to have particular regard to innate factors such as their physical and neurological make-up and their own special measure of intelligence. Except as a matter of degree, however, this cannot be said to represent an entirely novel approach upon the part of psycho-analysts.

Concept of the unconscious prior to Freud

A charge recurrently made against Freud is that he did not discover the unconscious, and that long before he began the investigations that led to the foundation of psycho-analysis, the concept was to be found expressed or reflected in the writings of philosophers and poets.[2]

This is unfair, as Freud expressly repudiated any claim to be the first person to discover the unconscious, and acknowledged that he had been anticipated by the philosopher, Schopenhauer (1788-1860). Nevertheless he maintained, and not incorrectly, that he had been the first to discover a scientific method for studying the unconscious. In any event the point appears somewhat academic as the psycho-analytical concept of the unconscious is radically different from the idea of the unconscious, as espoused, expressly or impliedly, by pre-Freudian philosophers and poets, and ranges over wider areas of the behaviour and mental life of human beings.

Thus if we go as far back as Aristotle, we can if we like say that a notion of unconscious mental phenomena is to be found in dim and germ-like form in his theory of the soul and of knowledge, but this hardly bears comparison with the developed concept of the unconscious according to psycho-analytical theory.

For Leibniz (1646-1716) and certain philosophers who followed him, the notion of the unconscious was relevant in regard to the doctrine of unconscious perceptions, meaning perceptions which a person may undoubtedly have but of which he is not aware. For example, a person listening to the noise of the sea may hear

[2] For a comprehensive, detailed study of theories and concepts regarding the unconscious held by philosophers and others before Freud, see L. L. Whyte, *The Unconscious Before Freud*, New York, 1960.

the noise of each wave, but have no more than an unconscious perception of separate waves. This is the idea of the unconscious in a very limited context.[3]

Two philosophers who wrote in the nineteenth century, J. F. Herbart (1776-1841) and Karl von Hartmann (1842-1906), dealt with the unconscious upon a wider and more specific basis than their predecessors. Herbart put forward the notion of a conflict between conscious and unconscious ideas. To illustrate the range of von Hartmann's thought on the subject, he made significant references to the 'unconscious will', and to the unconscious 'in sexual love', 'in feeling', and 'in instinct'. Yet withal these were views of the unconscious within limited, speculative philosophic frames of reference, far different from Freud's theory, developed not in the capacity of a philosopher, but as a scientist who had already engaged in skilled research, and working with materials derived from actual clinical experience and with the data revealed in descriptive anthropological literature.

The scope of the psycho-analytical concept of the unconscious

Broadly speaking, the psycho-analytical concept of the unconscious covers mental processes, mental forces, and mental phenomena of which the subject is not consciously aware. The expression 'broadly speaking' is used because as yet there has emerged no definitive, comprehensive delimitation of the scope of the unconscious to which all psycho-analysts will subscribe. For one thing, the extent to which such processes, forces, and phenomena are unconscious, and the degree to which they remain unconscious, vary from individual to individual. Then also, certain mental processes can, according to the circumstances and according to the individual, be either conscious or unconscious. Illustrations are the wish to draw attention to oneself, and the process of identification. With regard to the first, in a woman of fashion, the wish to draw attention to oneself may be perfectly conscious, while in the case of hysterical persons, this wish, while sometimes conscious, may often be deeply unconscious. Similarly, with regard to identification, there may be quite conscious identification as when a boy looks to his father as an ideal or a student idolizes a particular professor. Or there can be unconscious identification, as when a young man, in boyhood

[3] The question of perception is nevertheless of some importance for psycho-analytical theory. See G. S. Klein in *Journal of the American Psycho-analytic Association,* Vol. 7 (1959), pp. 20-7.

intensely attached to his mother, unconsciously identifies himself with her to the extent of being unable to form a genuine heterosexual relationship.

It follows that the unconscious, as discussed in the theoretical works on psycho-analysis, tends to appear as a somewhat fluid concept. An exact, comprehensive, definition of the concept would be difficult, and, as is the case with certain concepts in other sciences, is not indispensable, either for practical or for theoretical purposes. A maxim familiar to lawyers seems here to be in point: 'When it is unnecessary to determine, it is necessary not to determine'. This is the more so since, under psycho-analytic doctrine, the unconscious operates dynamically in motivating or conditioning human behaviour and in its effect upon conscious mental processes. A descriptive formula is hardly appropriate for such a dynamic concept.

However, allowing for variations in individual cases, some of the contents of the unconscious may be noted. For psycho-analysts, perhaps the most important component is *repressed* material, and such material, as a matter of historical origin, can be largely traced back to the period of the individual's early childhood. The notion of repression is fundamental to a proper understanding of the concept of the unconscious. In essence, repression is the mental process of rejecting and excluding material from consciousness. In effect certain unwelcome instinctual impulses, memories, wishes, and fantasies, mainly related to early childhood, are kept out of consciousness because these are not in harmony with the superior demands of another part of the psyche. It is important to note that the subject-matter of repression can be not only impulses, wishes, and memories related to actual infantile experiences, but also fantasies of the child concerned, without any basis in reality other than their psychic existence. As a rule such fantasies must be connected to unwelcome impulses and urges. Something of the nature of an internal censorship operates, relegating undesirable impulses, wishes, memories, and fantasies to the unconscious layers of the mind, possibly by a multi-stage sequence. The 'censoring' is predominantly due to the operation of that inner part of the mind, the super-ego, discharging the functions of a conscience, and representing largely the mental heritage of parental authority, although the actual function of repression is discharged by that part of the mind, known as the ego, which, *inter alia,* controls perception and voluntary thought, is in contact with reality, and is oriented to the self-preservation of the individual (see Chapter III).

Repression can occur both when the unwelcome impulse, memory, or wish is aroused through external perception, or is of spontaneous origin. In the first instance, the process may be conscious, although later manifestations of repression may be unconscious. Essentially, repression involves a continuous expenditure of mental energy and is not confined to a single occasion.

Originally, Freud did not distinctly differentiate the concept of repression from the concept of defence considered in Chapter III. For example, he used the German word *Abwehr* or 'defence', in the first instance to designate what he later called 'repression'. The word 'repression' was, however, more flexible to encompass the processes of censoring which he encounted in his clinical work, and this led to the supersession of the term 'defence' in that connection.[4] Later, the distinction between the two mechanisms was clarified.[5] This early absence of differentiation is understandable, for, as will be seen, repression, or some like process, is present side by side with the various defence mechanisms.

One of the major problems concerning repression is that of its relationship to the unconscious. In other words, what are the nature and content of the material repressed, and then embedded in the unconscious?

Freud indicated that although repressed material finds its way to the unconscious, not all material in the unconscious is necessarily repressed. The unconscious may conceivably contain some non-repressed material, and the descriptive anthropological literature suggests that this could be related to the instincts, and to particular sexual and non-sexual symbols. One illustration is that of the water-urine symbolism which seems to be common to the unconscious of human beings on a universal scale, and is reflected in statues and fountains throughout the world, and in long-standing legends and folklore. Havelock Ellis regarded an interest in urine as a basic, innate element of sexuality, and not necessarily a deviance or perversion. He made a detailed study of what he called the 'Undinist' aspect of sexual psychology. (The word is based on 'Undine', the female water sprite according to legend.) Then, as shown in dreams, the symbol of water by itself is a representation of birth

[4] See Robert Waelder in *The Psychoanalytical Quarterly,* Vol. XXXVI (1967), pp. 8, 29. For Freud's early, fluid use of the two terms, see the example in his paper of 1896, 'Further Remarks on the Neuro-Psychoses of Defence', *Complete Psychological Works of S. Freud,* Vol. III, p. 175.

[5] This was done by Freud in 1926 in his study, *Inhibitions, Symptoms and Anxiety* (English translation by Alix Strachey) London 1936, pp. 154-5.

or a re-birth, and this belongs in a primal sense to deep layers of the unconscious. It is difficult to attribute the presence of such a symbol in the unconscious in all cases to repression. The urine-fire relationship may be another such example of a non-repressed, unconscious symbolism, and the author inclines to the view that the symbol of fire in itself is part of the universal unconscious heritage of mankind.

These are examples of inherently unconscious non-repressed material. But experience suggests that the unconscious may be a repository also of impressions and patterns that have been individually lived through by a person, without being of an inherent nature, and without ever having been repressed. A good example, perhaps, is that of a category of patient who has come under the notice of most practising psycho-analysts; one with a wish to be mothered. This wish can in some individuals be unconscious, and unrepressed, often linked with a closely related unconscious attachment to the mother's breast. Another case of non-inherent, non-repressed unconscious impressions is that of certain persons with highly developed artistic senses, the unremembered foundations of which were laid in very early childhood through living, for example, in a house which contained beautiful paintings and works of art, or for a short time in a musical milieu. Such unconscious impressions may have a life-long influence upon conscious thought and behaviour, without the individual necessarily being aware of their original source.

One can perhaps go further and urge that the unconscious may be a storehouse of a great variety of impressions, thoughts, and experiences belonging to the first years of infancy and which have been banished from consciousness, not because of the operation of a process of repression, but by reason of some general law affecting the psyche of children after the fifth or sixth year of life. This point of the failure of memory regarding infantile life has been well brought out by Anna Freud[6] in her classical lectures, *Introduction to Psycho-Analysis for Teachers*. First published in England in 1931, they showed to what extent the feelings and experiences of infancy may be pushed altogether from recollection. Some impressions and events may be practically buried for ever, inaccessible to consciousness. Parents who have tried to jog the memory of their

[6] Daughter of Sigmund Freud, and herself very distinguished in the field of psycho-analysis. The point of infantile amnesia was classically dealt with by Freud himself in *Three Essays on the Theory of Sexuality* (1905).

children regarding happenings in the first five years of life, which could not possibly have been repressed in the sense postulated by psycho-analysts, and who have found their children suffering from a state of virtual amnesia regarding these events, will not need to be convinced on the matter. It has been suggested that such unconscious, non-repressed mental material, belonging to early infancy, must be distinguished from that part of the unconscious produced by repression. The former is of phenomenological, but not of dynamic value, exercising no influence whatever on the consciousness of the persons concerned in puberty. This may be true of some but not all non-repressed unconscious material appertaining to early infancy. Time and again, it will be found in the course of an analysis that unremembered infantile experiences, not themselves subject to repression, have played some role, symbolically or otherwise, in relation to the more important repressed wishes and feelings.

The preconscious

In this connection, Freud preferred to reserve the term 'unconscious' for the dynamically unconscious repressed material, and to use 'preconscious' for that part of the unconscious which is only of descriptive significance, affirming that in the dynamic sense there is only one unconscious. Hence, in theory, preconscious mental material could be accessible to consciousness, because of its non-repressed nature, and the lack of resistance to bringing it to the surface. Ordinary methods of introspection, or of refreshing memory, might bring material to consciousness without the difficulties experienced in the course of psycho-analytical therapy, at times when repressed material requires to be brought to the surface.[7]

Court-room experience with the examination and cross-examination of witnesses suggests that there may be formidable difficulties in bringing back to consciousness events or feelings embedded in the unconscious memory, and which are preconscious in the sense of being non-repressed, and exercising no influence on the conscious mind. Even the use of contemporary written documents in order to refresh memory may not be sufficient to re-evoke

[7] According to Hartmann, the preconscious functions more or less as conscious activities do, and can become conscious without having to overcome 'powerful counterforces'. See Sidney Hook (ed.), *Psycho-analysis . . .* , pp. 5-6.

prior happenings or feelings in the conscious mind of a witness. Unpleasant events may simply not be recalled, and in the perspective of time, the identical contemporary shade or intensity of feeling cannot be recaptured. Freud, however, expressly stated that the term 'preconscious' referred to the unconscious only in a descriptive sense, and not in a dynamic sense. So in distinguishing the preconscious from the dynamic concept of the unconscious, he was doubtless thinking primarily in clinical terms of making a patient aware of unconscious, repressed material as distinct from such unconscious material as had not contributed to the patient's illness.

This should not lead one to believe that Freud meant that preconscious material is of no significance whatever in the course of a psycho-analytical treatment. In an analysis, a patient is required at all times to comply with the fundamental rule of giving free expression to whatever may come into his mind. These freely expressed thoughts may include preconscious material which has happened to enter the mind and has thus become conscious. Moreover, at a particular phase of the treatment, it may well be that such preconscious material becomes of some importance, viewed against the background of the patient's emotional relationship to the psycho-analyst—or transference situation, as it is called—the handling of which is so vital for cure.

Character of the unconscious

Thus the psycho-analytical concept of the unconscious is above all a dynamic one. This repressed inner world of man does not remain in a compartment and does not cease to influence, shape and condition conscious attitudes, feelings and desires. One may go further and say that, under special circumstances, it may be the genesis of other unconscious processes, as when the individual is member of a nation under a leader subscribing to an ideology of aggression against another nation or nations. By an unconscious process of regression, reproducing the infantile characteristics of the original development of conscience in early childhood, the leader and the ideology of aggression become an external substitute for the inner conscience, so that an ordinarily peaceful individual may regard violence as permissible.[8]

While dynamic in this sense, the unconscious has also a special

[8] For discussion of this process, in the context of war and peace, see Robert Waelder, *Psychological Aspects of War and Peace,* Geneva Research Centre Studies 1939.

character of inflexibility and relative unalterability. This is well reflected in the difficulties of psycho-analytical therapy. The popular assumption of a cure by psycho-analysis is that immediately the patient becomes aware, by himself or through the interpretation of the analyst, of the repressed unconscious wishes or thoughts which have produced his troubles, there is a kind of magically automatic recovery from his illness. Such a view of the therapeutic process is an illusory over-simplification.

Consciousness is not penetrated except as the result of a thorough 'working-through' of the unconscious material. This produces its own phenomenon of an unconscious resistance to recovery. Then there are gradations of depth in which the repressed material is buried. The first few weeks of treatment may be adequate only to cope with the upper layers. This is well shown by the therapeutic difficulties of dealing with certain repressed homosexual wishes, which have unconscious manifestations ranging from immediately beneath the surface of consciousness to the deepest strata of the inner mind.

According to psycho-analytical theory, such rigidity and intractability are due to the foundations of the unconscious being laid in early childhood. This is dealt with in the next, and subsequent chapters.

Related to the inflexibility of the unconscious is its quality of 'timelessness'. The repressed material—wishes, fantasies, and feelings—does not appear in the unconscious in any chronological order, and each repressed component remains fixed in the form in which it entered the unconscious. The buried conflicts and impulses retain their character to such an extent that they are untouched by the mainstream of the continuing development of the subject's own conscious personality. So, in this general sense, the unconscious may be regarded as almost archaic. Nevertheless, the order of time may have some influence upon the relative extent of the depth and fixation of each component of the repressed unconscious material, so that it is possible for the repressed mental experiences of earlier phases of infancy to be less accessible to consciousness than those which, by force of repression, came to enter the unconscious at a later stage of infancy.

Conflict and the unconscious

Freud's dynamic approach to the unconscious rested upon his acceptance of what was, for him, the empirically proved hypothesis that determinism[9] applied to mental phenomena generally. This deterministic approach comes out most strongly in his classical study of 1901, *The Psychopathology of Everyday Life*. Here he formulated the law that shortcomings in psychological functioning, for example slips of the tongue, misreadings of words, and lapses of memory of an unintentional nature, can, upon the application of the psycho-analytical technique of investigation, be traced to motives or material appertaining to the unconscious. Such mental malfunctioning in the case of normal persons appeared to prove that the dynamic theory of the unconscious was not one which applied solely to persons suffering from neurotic disorders, although much of Freud's initial data-material had been derived from experience of these persons.

According to psycho-analytical theory the unconscious is neither necessarily homogeneous nor necessarily at rest. This is true for all persons. This view has not found favour with some critics, including philosophers, but remains a fundamental of psycho-analysis. Hence, there may be conflicts: (a) within the unconscious itself, as between inconsistent or irreconcilable wishes, motives, and other components of the inner mind; (b) as between some conscious wish or attitude, on the one hand, and a wish, motive, or feeling of an unconscious nature, on the other hand. The subject of conflict is also mentioned in Chapter III. The fact that there are such conflicts of the category (b) is proof of another characteristic of the unconscious, according to psycho-analytical theory, namely, that the unconscious does not necessarily operate alone, but may work with other mental forces and processes.

Instincts and symbols, and the unconscious

This chapter may be rounded off by briefly dealing with the query, raised by some philosophers and anthropologists, whether the instincts and sexual symbols are to be characterized as belonging to the unconscious. It is not easy to give a satisfactory answer to this question, a full treatment of which cannot be attempted in this book.

So far as the instincts are concerned, in a broad and loose sense, they appertain to the unconscious. But they are reflected in a multiplicity of manifestations and components, which according to the individual concerned can be conscious or unconscious. So there

[9] According to Dr Heinz Hartmann, Freud was a 'strict determinist'. See Sidney Hook (ed.), *Psychoanalysis . . .* , p. 8.

are persons who have repressed unconscious wishes of an aggressive or masochistic or homosexual nature, while there can at the same time be also persons possessing aggressive or masochistic or homosexual wishes which are quite conscious and unrepressed.

It seems clear, however, that one instinct must be treated as primarily of an unconscious character. That is the death instinct which, as mentioned in the preceding chapter, was postulated by Freud.

As in the case of the instincts, there is a like difficulty in predicating whether or not sexual symbols, such as phallic and vaginal ones, belong to the unconscious. This again depends to a large extent upon the individuals concerned. Thus, the data in descriptive anthropological literature (and the author's own experience of Australian aboriginals in certain areas) suggest that some races, living in a primitive manner close to the earth, can be very conscious of sexual symbolism. But for many persons who belong to highly educated, highly urbanized communities, sexual symbolism may for various reasons (one of which is perhaps a high degree of repression) be unconscious. However, the largely unconscious nature of sexual symbols and of the process of sexual symbolism is reflected in the formation of dreams (see Chapter VI), and of their content, as well as in the special nature of the symptoms of certain neuroses such as the obsessional neuroses (see Chapter VII).

Dreams provide countless illustrations of unconscious symbolization, the male genital organ being represented by such images as sticks, umbrellas, poles, trees, daggers, pistols, and watering cans; erection by flying in aircraft, and going up in lifts; the pubic hair by woods, forests, and shrubberies; and the female genitalia by such representations as pits, caves, pockets, jars, rooms, and gates.[10] In the case of the obsessional neuroses, one of Freud's most famous examples was that of the young woman who, prior to retiring each night, regularly observed a painstaking ritual of positioning flower-pots and vases so that they could not possibly fall, and of removing all clocks from her room. The flower-pots, vases, and clocks were unconscious symbols of the female genitalia, and the compulsive ritual was in part an expression of repressed sexual wishes, in part a defence against them.[11]

Unconscious symbolization may also involve the representation

[10] See Freud, *A General Introduction to Psychoanalysis* (English translation by Joan Riviere), New York 1943, pp. 138-9.

[11] Ibid., pp. 234-8.

in a disguised form of words or phrases, possessing some emotional or traumatic significance for the personality. An illustration of this, given by Freud, as early as 1893,[12] concerned a patient suffering from the physically inexplicable hysterical symptom of pains in the right heel. Elucidation of the symptom revealed its connection to a deep-rooted fear of the patient that, upon her first appearance in society, she might not find herself on a right footing.

[12] In a Lecture at Vienna on 11 January 1893, 'On the Psychical Mechanism of Hysterical Phenomena', *Complete Psychological Works of S. Freud,* Vol. III, pp. 27, 34.

Chapter III

THE STRUCTURAL THEORY OF PERSONALITY—EGO, ID AND SUPER-EGO

The structural theory of personality propounded by Freud and refined by psycho-analytical theory, conceives the mind as a tripartite arrangement composed of the ego, the id, and the super-ego. Sometimes these components are referred to as 'divisions' of the mind, sometimes as 'systems', sometimes as 'provinces', and sometimes as 'groups of functions'. All of these expressions are in a sense correct, and useful pointers.

This structural representation of personality has been considered to stand the test of time, and as offering certain theoretical and clinical advantages. According to a distinguished psycho-analyst,[1] the most important advantage is probably that the demarcation lines are geared to man's typical conflicts with the outside world, with his instinctual drives, and with his conscience. The paramount importance of these conflicts is central to psycho-analysis.

As in the case of the psycho-analytic concept of the unconscious, the structural theory reflects a dynamic approach to personality. According to it there is interaction between the ego, the id, and the super-ego. 'Interaction' perhaps conveys more than the word 'interdependence' the idea that the structural theory is concerned with the dynamics of personality rather than with a static and phenomenological conception of the mind. Indeed, the theory treats the ego, the id, and the super-ego as being mental systems primarily of a functional nature, each being directed to certain goals or fulfilling certain purposes. Nor is there any underlying assumption that the mind is patterned in this way because of some

[1] Dr Heinz Hartmann in Sidney Hook (ed.), *Psychoanalysis . . .* , p. 10.

dominant biological necessity that the normal state of personality should be one of integration. The facts may be to the contrary, for in the interaction of the ego, the id, and the super-ego, there can be conflicts arising out of inconsistency or irreconcilability of the mental forces or processes operating in each sector. Consistently, the structural theory does not regard these sectors of the mind as having a sharply separate character.

Broad definitions

Before dealing with the ego, the id, and the super-ego in detail, it may be as well to give the following broad definitions, which must be read in the context of the subsequent fuller analyses.

Ego: The largely conscious part of the mind, concerned with perception, rational thought and conduct,[2] and adjustment to reality,[3] and which is in a sense oriented to self-preservation of the person. The ego is also the seat of the psyche's defences against undesirable impulses, and against mental pain and anxiety.

Id: The id is that unconscious part of the mind which provides a storehouse for the basic instinctive urges and drives of personality, being those demanding gratification or satisfaction, irrespective of rational considerations.

Super-ego: The super-ego is that division of the mind described by Anna Freud[4] as an inner 'court of judgment'. It represents an internal incorporation of the authority of parents and parent-figures, constituting the source of inner moral dictates and prohibitions, as well as of standards and ideals established internally, and conditioning the ambitions and aspirations of the individual concerned. The super-ego may be regarded as another term for the conscience, or perhaps more precisely it may be treated as discharging the functions of a conscience.

The ego

Although the ego is primarily the conscious part of the mind, it is the seat also of some unconscious forces; e.g. resistance to recovery

[2] Borrowing the nomenclature of brain physiology, the ego may be characterized as involving 'centralization of functional control'. See Dr Heinz Hartmann in Sidney Hook (ed.), *Psychoanalysis . . .* , pp. 9-10.

[3] The ego is indeed said to serve the so-called 'reality principle'. Reality includes not only external environment, but the physical characteristics (e.g. stamina, and athletic capacity) of the person concerned.

[4] *Introduction to Psycho-Analysis for Teachers: Four Lectures*, London 1931, p. 94.

in the case of neurotic disorder. As Freud has pointed out, the ego is in control of voluntary movement, and has also to deal with the main tasks of the individual in relation to environment—self-preservation, adaptation and adjustment to the physical world, and coping with the demands of society. According to psycho-analytical theory, it is said to act in conformity with the 'reality principle', which means that it accepts restraints, and may abstain from pleasure or incur pain with a view to some advantageous end-result. The ego is often described as a 'problem-solving agency', as though it were a concrete entity. It is better to think of the ego as a theoretical concept corresponding to certain consciously performed, mainly integrative functions of the mind. One duty of the ego that should not be overlooked is that of adjustment to the demands of the id, and of giving due weight to the unconscious dictates and prohibitions of the super-ego.

More elaborate attention has been given to the ego by post-Freudian psycho-analysis, although the importance of the ego was never disregarded by Freud and his collaborators. There has emerged a special body of doctrine, with the alternative titles of 'psycho-analytic ego psychology' and 'analytic ego psychology'. Perhaps it may appear strange that psycho-analysts should be devoting so much attention to the analysis of a largely conscious division of the mind, since the general impression is that psycho-analysis is concerned with depth-analysis of the mind. There are two reasons for the trend to close examination of the ego. First, parts of the ego, and processes within it may be, and often are, unconscious. To this extent they are legitimately a subject for investigation by psycho-analysts according to the tradition that unconscious forces are a proper concern of psycho-analysis. Secondly, the strengthening of the ego is important for the therapeutic side of psycho-analysis, enabling it to grapple with the demands of the unconscious, as these are made conscious. Hence a scientific understanding of the factors which contribute to the weakness or to the strength of the ego is a matter of the utmost interest to all psycho-analysts. To this extent, progress in the development of psycho-analytic ego psychology may be expected to be of considerable therapeutic significance in stressing the need for attention to the ego. It ought not be assumed, however, that the importance of the ego in the clinical domain was overlooked by analysts prior to 1939.

A number of new concepts and new hypotheses have been developed by those who have made contributions in the field of psycho-analytic ego psychology. The result has been to open new perspectives in both the theoretical and clinical areas of psycho-analysis, and to provide new tools for the elaboration of a more adequate methodology of the subject. As has been noted: 'ego psychology represents a more balanced consideration of the biological and the social and cultural aspects of human behaviour',[5] enabling cultural phenomena to be studied in psycho-analysis in their biological context, and biological phenomena in relation to the socio-cultural environment. Apart from possible contributions to the understanding of the central nervous system, these advances in ego psychology may prove of value to those working in the growing field of human biology which is related to human adaptability, one of the central purposes of the ego.

Some of the more striking concepts developed with regard to the ego have been as follows:

(*a*) *The defence mechanisms of the ego*

The notion of an array of defence mechanisms available to the ego to protect it from the inner dangers of the instinctual urges, sexual and aggressive, was expounded by Anna Freud in her notable study of 1936, *The Ego and the Mechanisms of Defence*. Sigmund Freud had given these defences prior, but not so detailed, thought.[6] Indeed, it may perhaps be said that the concept of defence had been foreshadowed much earlier during the period 1893-1896, when the first foundations of psycho-analysis were being laid. Thus, there are some indications of the concept of defence in two papers by Freud of 1894 and 1896 respectively entitled 'The Neuro-Psychoses of Defence'[7] and 'Further Remarks on the Neuro-Psychoses of Defence'.[8] In both papers, though, the precise distinction between repression and defence was not clarified. The concept of defence mechanisms of the ego really represents an extension from the position that repression is the primary technique employed by the ego for banishing to the unconscious those tendencies, thoughts, and impulses, deemed unacceptable. Illustrations of defence mechanisms, having their seat in the ego, are such pro-

[5] Dr Heinz Hartmann, in Sidney Hook (ed.), *Psychoanalysis* . . . , pp. 14-5.

[6] In 1926, in *Inhibitions, Symptoms and Anxiety* he reverted to the old term of 'defence', and clarified the distinction between defence techniques, on the one hand, and repression, on the other. See the English translation by Alix Strachey, London 1936, pp. 154-5.

[7] *Complete Psychological Works of S. Freud,* Vol. III, pp. 45-61.

[8] Ibid., pp. 162-185.

cesses as rationalization (a reasoned justification of some act or symptom, conditioned by an unconscious urge repugnant to the person concerned), projection (attribution to another person of an inner attitude, wish, or impulse, felt by the projecting person to be repugnant), regression (retreat to an earlier phase of development, to avoid coping with mature impulses), auto-erotic thinking or imagination (acting out sexual impulses in the mind), and 'undoing' (a process normally expressed in the determination to treat some act or event as if it had not occurred).

According to psycho-analytic doctrine, the concept of defence mechanism, in the strict sense, does not apply to resistance by the ego to the adversities of external reality, but only to a defence against the danger of inner urges, both sexual and aggressive. Nor does the concept of defence mechanism involve any implication that such urges are to be minimized; the very word 'defence' suggests otherwise. It is however possible for a defence mechanism to become conditioned in such manner as to be 'conflict-free' in certain instances. The mechanism of reaction-formation provides a good example. Thus a person with insecurity due to repressed homosexual wishes may react excessively in the opposite direction by adopting a manner in public which is bold and unabashed, instead of insecure. He may behave in this way, by force of conditioning, without necessarily reacting against an insecurity due to repressed urges.

As has been pointed out by some psycho-analysts,[9] the defence mechanisms of the ego are not invariably of a pathological nature. In certain cases, they can fulfil normal educational or cultural purposes. For example, the mechanism of projection may sharpen a person's insight and provide encouragement and stimulation towards achievement.

It is claimed that repression, or something akin to repression accompanies any one or more of the defence mechanisms of the ego. An illustration is that of reaction-formation, where repressed wishes occasion the process of reaction itself, except in those cases where the reaction-formation is 'conflict-free'.

An important point is that the defence mechanisms are, so to speak, patterned processes of the ego of a particular individual. They represent stereotyped, automatic, repetitive, and standardized responses. Being characteristic of the individual himself, they are

def. mech.

[9] See, e.g. P. J. Van der Leeuw, 'On the Development of the Concept of Defence', *International Journal of Psycho-Analysis,* Vol. 52 (1972), p. 51, at p. 56.

predictable.[10] This fact is of clinical significance, since a person's defence mechanisms identify traits for which therapy may be necessary if the mechanisms are pathological, in the same way as other pathological conditions peculiar to that person. As has been pointed out,[11] this 'added a new dimension to analytic work'.

'Ego restriction' and 'ego distortion': The process of so-called 'ego restriction' is one kind of mechanism of defence of the ego that has received special attention from psycho-analysts. This means that the individual concerned simply renounces interest in an area of his ambitions that may expose him to neurotic disorder; for example change of career, or withdrawal from matrimonial life. What are the values here involved?[12] In one sense, it may be said that the person gives up too easily the struggle with reality. On the other hand, the solution is a practical one, in the sense that it involves acceptance of reality and mitigation of suffering.

The concept of 'ego distortion' is not quite the same as that of 'ego restriction', and only in a broad sense can be regarded as a defence mechanism of the ego. By change of personality, a neurosis is warded off. No doubt also when a person is told that he must live with an actual neurosis without being able to cure it, just as people sometimes have to live with and endure compromises, this involves a form of ego distortion.

(*b*) *The sensate ego*

According to the concept of the sensate ego, the ego is the focus of the sensations of the personality, including particularly self-awareness and sense of identity. How far the sensate ego is related to the unconscious is a matter of disagreement, but according to some, a segment of it is conscious, and uninfluenced by the unconscious. The concept of the sensate ego may prove to be of significance for the understanding of certain mental disorders, ranging from the mild category of feelings of insecurity and lack of identity with the environment to the severe psychoses which have to date proved unamenable to psycho-analytical treatment. Leaving clinical phenomena aside, the author's impression from court-room experience is that the concept may have value in the identification of cases of mental disorder, bordering on schizophrenia.

10 Robert Waelder in *The Psychoanalytical Quarterly*, Vol. XXXVI (1967), p. 1, at pp. 30-1.

11 *Ibid.*, p. 32.

12 For an interesting article on values in psycho-analysis, see I. Ramzy, 'The Place of Values in Psycho-Analysis', *International Journal of Psycho-Analysis*, Vol. 46 (1965), pp. 97-106.

(*c*) *Autonomy of the ego*

According to the concept of ego autonomy, the ego has an automony resting on the innate processes of memory, perception, and motor action, which were originally independent of conflict with, or adaptation to the environment, or demands of the unconscious. This point of view is relevant for the purpose of explaining how, historically, in infancy and later, the ego becomes differentiated from the id, and recognizes that the ego may undergo its own characteristic development subsequently, while also some degree of relative autonomy in relation to the environment may continue. This represents only a broad picture of the theory of the autonomous ego, but it seems to have implications of value for human biology in general, while it may also explain failures in therapy.

(*d*) *Ego strength*

The concept of ego strength seems, currently, to have more practical value than other concepts of psycho-analytical ego psychology. Ego strength alone may not necessarily be decisive in a patient's struggle for recovery, but it can contribute to that result, and in any event can operate to mitigate suffering. In the early history of psycho-analysis, the process of free association of thoughts by a patient was thought to have an effect by way of catharsis through removal of unpleasant or repugnant thoughts in the unconscious or preconscious, so that to this extent such catharsis could contribute to the strength of the ego. A central aspect of ego strength is ability to cope with aggressive instincts. If the ego allows aggression to become internalized by repression, its strength is diminished; if it can find a way of discharging or neutralizing aggressive energy, it is not subject to enfeeblement through the internal aggressive energy being turned against it, primarily through the absence of alternative outlet. To some extent, this explains why work may aid neurotic patients to recover, through the absorption of aggressive energy. It could also be maintained that work strengthens the innate processes of memory, perception, reasoning, and motor action, which underlie the autonomy of the ego.

(*e*) *The adaptive ego*

Dr Heinz Hartmann is credited with having first emphasized the adaptive role of the ego, in 1937. It is said that the adaptation may take passive and active forms. The concept of the adaptive ego found an echo—if this is the right word—in 1939 in Freud's

Outline of Psycho-Analysis, where he referred to the ego as performing functions of self-preservation by different processes, including that of 'dealing with moderate stimuli (through adaptation).'[13] It may be legitimately claimed, however, that the concept of the adaptive ego had been in the forefront of Freud's thoughts for some years, but without receiving elaboration in detail. For example, the concept is reflected in his theory that in the case of neurotic anxiety, the ego responds to the inner dangers of the instinctual urges with an anxiety-signal (see Chapter V). Such anxiety-signal may properly be regarded as an adaptative response of the ego.[14] It follows also that, insofar as the ego is the seat of purposive processes, such processes may have impact in the psychic domain, as distinct from the physical world of external reality.

According to psycho-analytic doctrine, the ego acts in conformity with the 'reality principle', as a general rule. This would seem to be applicable primarily in relation to *external* matters or events. In his latest formulation in 1939, dealing with the *internal* domain, Freud postulated that the 'ego pursues pleasure and seeks to avoid unpleasure',[15] and in that connection he had in mind the process by which the ego responds to an increase in 'unpleasure' by an anxiety-signal.

Distinction between the self and the ego

In recent psycho-analytical theories, some emphasis has been laid upon the distinction between the self, on the one hand, and the ego, on the other.[16] The self is conceived as entirely a psychological structure with a specific individuality lacking in the ego, acting predominantly in accordance with the 'pleasure principle' in relation to external reality. The ego is seen as primarily a 'body ego'—a system based on the physiology of the person concerned, and observing the 'reality principle' in relationship to the physical world.

[13] See *An Outline of Psycho-Analysis* (English translation by James Strachey), London 1949, p. 2.

[14] The anxiety-signal theory was propounded by Freud in 1926 in *Inhibitions, Symptoms and Anxiety,* pp. 111-112. For a reference to an 'adaptive response' in regard to the anxiety-signal, see Robert Waelder, in *The Psychoanalytic Quarterly,* Vol. XXXVI (1967), p. 17.

[15] See *An Outline of Psycho-Analysis* (English translation by James Strachey), London 1949, p. 3.

[16] See, e.g., D. C. Levin, 'The Self: a Contribution to its Place in Theory and Technique', *International Journal of Psycho-Analysis,* Vol. 50 (1969), pp. 41-51; and Robert C. Bak, same journal, Vol. 51 (1970), p. 257.

The distinction is helpful as clarifying the sense of identity, the search for which is claimed to be characteristic of some of those persons afflicted with inner insecurity. Identity is considered to be a derivative of self. One of the functions of the ego is doubtless the achievement of harmony with the self.[17]

The id

By contrast with the ego, the id has no direct contact with the outside world. According to psycho-analytical theory, it serves to provide psychic energy for the whole personality, such energy flowing from a fusion of the two primal instinctive urges, sexual and aggressive, compounded in varying proportions. Impulses and processes within the id operate pursuant to the 'pleasure principle'.[18] Immediate gratification is sought of an urge or wish pertaining to the id, irrespective of the consequences rationally considered. Freud affirmed that the id obeys the pleasure principle as inexorable. The id is archaic, knowing nothing of a self-preserving urge.

Are there any perceptions within the id? Freud seems to have thought that the id responded with sensitivity to fluctuations in the tension of its two instinctual components. But the id has no capacity to tolerate tension. The strength of the instinctual drives in the id can vary from person to person, as can the relative strengths of the id and the ego. An id that is over-strong in relation to the ego may create the same problems as the reality of a harsh environment.

Although eighty years have passed since the very earliest foundations of psycho-analysis were laid, the id still remains relatively unexplorable and obscure. Perhaps with fresh advances in our knowledge of the central nervous system and progress in the field of human biology, new insights will become possible. Since civilization and human behaviour depend upon the control of the id, there are few projects more important than to uncover its secrets.

The super-ego

Psycho-analysts regard the super-ego as less mysterious than the id. A great deal is known about how it comes to be formed, although a number of obscurities remain.

17 The distinction between ego and self is expressed in the commonly stated proposition that the ego 'has the task of self-preservation'; see Freud's *An Outline of Psycho-Analysis*, p. 2.

18 It can perhaps be more precisely put that conformity to this principle involves seeking a maximum of pleasure and a minimum of pain.

It appears to be the general view of psycho-analysts, based on the experience of child analysis, on clinical data obtained from analysis of adults, and taken in conjunction with the results of observation of young children, that the super-ego becomes established in the inner mind through a mixed process of identification by the child with parents and parent-figures, and of internalized acceptance of the attitudes and wishes of such parents and parent-figures. But this is a multi-stage process. The first phase, in which the authority of a parental nature is exercised *externally,* is as important as any. Then the young child, in the second and third years of life, realises his dependence[19] on parents for food and love, and at the same time their powers of correction. He comes to recognize what is right and wrong in the opinion of the parents, and it is at this stage when a feeling of guilt will first consciously be experienced after committing some act considered wrong by the parents.

This leads to a time when internalization begins. Usually by the end of the fifth year, the nucleus of the super-ego has crystallized. Then new parent-figures, teachers and the like, aided by further identifications, by the acceptance of authority, and by the inculcation of moral ideas, complete the process of formation of the super-ego. In the case of the majority of persons, the process of incorporation of authoritarian ideas and prohibitory mandates may continue, if not throughout life, for a long time into adulthood.

With different individuals, the sequence of the steps of identification, and introjection of the inner 'court of judgment' need not be the same during the period of early childhood. Some parents are more authoritarian than others, some are more prone to use physical correction, and some give their children a free rein. None the less, it has been a matter of clinical experience that an oppressive super-ego does not necessarily mean that the subject's parents were severe toward him during his early childhood; often the contrary has been the case. The degree of severity of the super-ego in certain instances remains a problem, which seems to bring into account factors special to the individual concerned.

Various explanations have been offered. Although not propounded specifically to account for the stern nature of the super-ego, the general 'Oedipal' theory of its formation would go far in this direction. Under this theory, the super-ego is regarded as

[19] This long dependence of the child upon a parent or parents, to the extent that it conditions the process of formation of the super-ego, may be regarded as a biological root of this part of the unconscious; cf Dr Heinz Hartmann in Sidney Hook (ed.), *Psychoanalysis . . .* , p. 10.

predominantly a heritage of the Oedipus complex. This complex is supposed to involve a little boy in his relations with his parents. The boy, resentful of the father monopolizing the mother's love, suffers from death wishes directed against the father. In the child's fantasies there is a fear that the father will punish him for such wishes. This threat of punishment by the father merges with the process of identification, contributing to the formation of the super-ego. Hence the authoritarian character of the super-ego is established.

There is much cogent clinical material and data from the descriptive anthropological literature to support the Oedipal theory regarding the super-ego. On the other hand, there are individual clinical cases showing the absence of any Oedipal situation, but rather a very strong love for the father in infancy, coupled with resentment directed against the mother for reasons such as giving more attention to the other children. Certain anthropologists have denied the validity of the Oedipal theory for indigenous communities, particularly those without a monogamous culture (see Chapter IV).

Another explanation for the severity of the super-ego is that in infancy aggression may not find proper outlets, may become internalized, and then in association with the super-ego, be turned against the ego. Some writers are prepared to go so far as to state that the internalization of aggression is an essential condition for the formation of the super-ego. This is a bold hypothesis which, if true, would itself raise further problems. However, it is affirmed that the basic energy which sustains the super-ego has its origins in the id, of which one component is the aggressive drive.

From clinical experience, some psycho-analysts have ventured the opinion that an especially severe super-ego, involving strong feeling of guilt, may be due to the absence of physical correction by the parents during infancy. This proposition suggests that physical correction of a young child, far from producing in the child aggression which becomes internalized, may have exactly the opposite result.

Some characteristics of the super-ego

The super-ego has a quality of resistance to alteration. This confirms the importance of the early years of childhood in controlling the growth of personality. Intense effort is necessary in psychoanalytical therapy not only to diminish the severity of the super-ego, but to bring about the desired result of an ego which is on terms with it. The object of therapy is not complete excision of the super-ego, which would seem an almost impossible task for psycho-analyst or psychiatrist, but to bring conscious enlightenment to the patient so that he is liberated from an unreasonable serfdom to unconscious exactions. In other words, the remedial aim is not perfection, but a more satisfactory equilibrium.

According to psycho-analytical theory, the energy which sustains the dynamic role of the super-ego is derived from the id, and this is consistent with the theory that the internalization of aggression is a condition of the formation of the super-ego. Because its energy comes from the id, some psycho-analysts would discard altogether the theory of identification with parents and parent-figures as contributing to the creation of the super-ego, and attribute its origins to aggression alone. There is disagreement, too, on the point whether the super-ego is or is not an independent creation. Some psycho-analysts continue to adhere to the view that it represents a specialized offshoot of the ego which, through development in early childhood, has obtained sufficient force to exist autonomously. This view explains some but not all problematical aspects.

Another theoretical controversy concerns the so-called 'ego-ideal', that is to say the standards or aspirations which condition personal behaviour and ambitions, and which have become internalized in the personality. Some psycho-analysts regard the ego-ideal as merged in the super-ego, while others deem that there is some advantage in maintaining a distinction between the two concepts. One reason given in support of the need for the distinction is that the primary feeling, in the event of a conflict between the ego and super-ego, is guilt, while in the case of a conflict between the ego and the ego-ideal, the emotional reaction is one of shame. Few would agree with this hypothesis, because a feeling of guilt is frequently associated with a failure to attain the ego-ideal, particularly where the ego-ideal corresponds with the actual or assumed wishes of parents or of parent-figures.

The super-ego, according to psycho-analytical theory, may demand both positive conduct and abstention from prohibited action. It includes both an 'ought' and an 'ought not'. Thus, it operates internally with the similar effect of laws ordained by the state. For this reason, there is much to be said for the view that to some extent the super-ego is self-preservative.[20]

20 By virtue of the process of identification with the parents, the super-ego also serves to facilitate the transmission from generation to generation of the culture of a group or groups.

While the super-ego functions unconsciously, its effects are felt consciously in the ego. Also a person may become conscious of its operation through psycho-analytic therapy. Yet one unconscious ingredient, which cannot be made clear to the conscious perception, may remain. That is an unconscious need for punishment. The latter is one of the most challenging enigmas of psycho-analysis, and is often regarded as underlying the absence of that will to recover which is one of the central factors in cure by psycho-analysis.

The super-ego is not necessarily only a source of aggression directed against the ego. If both in action and thought, irrespective of satisfying instinctive urges, the individual complies, faithfully and obediently, with the strictures and standards of the super-ego, he may be rewarded with self-love or self-esteem—narcissistic gratification.

Psycho-analytical literature conveys the impression that the super-ego always possesses some degree of severity, and the theories to the effect that aggression contributes to the formation of the super-ego reinforce the impression. However, it is not always true. There are many individuals with a low-degree super-ego, particularly among criminals and delinquents. Curiously, though, this class consists of many with a severe super-ego, unconsciously impelled to commit misdemeanours in order to satisfy an inner wish for punishment.

Nor should it be believed that the super-ego is for all persons an exclusive reservoir of morality, or that, because it represents the internalized voice of parents and parent-figures in the individual's infantile life, a person is always mature enough to need no other guidance. In many instances, it will be found that persons continue to need and to rely upon parent-figures all their lives. To a certain extent, the parent-figure represents a re-externalization of the super-ego. Since television has come to play such a dominant part in parliamentary elections, the phenomenon of a political leader fulfilling the image of a parent has become a matter of common observation. Politics is a sphere in which many of the fundamental truths of psycho-analysis receive empirical confirmation.

Conflict

In the preceding chapter, reference was made to the central importance of conflict in the context of the dynamic character of the unconscious. The notion of conflict is significant so far as it concerns the interaction of the ego, the id, and the super-ego.

Under psycho-analytic doctrine, conflict is 'a primary motivating force of behaviour'.[21] It is fundamental in the structure of the human personality, which does not easily remain stable under the subsistence of irreconcilable mental urges and tendencies, be they conscious or unconscious. In the case of certain persons, the intensity of the conflict may produce neurosis or illness. Conceivably, there is some neurological basis for an inability to tolerate the tension of inner conflicts without suffering symptoms, just as there is for the conflict between excitatory and inhibitory processes, as demonstrated according to Pavlov's researches concerning processes and tendencies in the central nervous sytem. The paradox, however, as shown by psycho-analytic doctrine concerning the resistance of the ego, is that while certain persons cannot bear inner conflicts without producing symptoms of pain or disturbance, their personality will manifest a strong and sometimes insuperable reluctance to permit resolution of the conflicts, or elimination of the underlying causes.

As pointed out earlier in this chapter, the ego may conflict with the outside world, with the instinctual drives of the id, and with the dictates and prohibitions of the super-ego. The expression 'outside world' embraces the socio-cultural environment in which the person may live, and in the case of neurosis, conflicts with such environment may contribute to exacerbating already existing inner conflicts. For this reason, if for no other, the possibility of such conflicts with the environment cannot be disregarded by either the theory or therapy of psycho-analysis.

Apart from conflict, the differentiation between ego and id is not a sharp one. There is constant interaction between the two.[22] Freud maintained that originally the whole of the psyche consisted of the id; then the ego evolved from the id, through certain material of the id becoming preconscious and being taken by the ego.[23] Thus, the ego-id relationship can, according to the person concerned, be concurrently one of conflict and of assimilation.

21 Cf. Sidney Hook (ed.), *Psychoanalysis . . .* , p. 10.

22 Or, as Robert Waelder has said, 'a constant traffic or migration back and forth' between them. See *The Psychoanalytic Quarterly*, Vol. XXXVI (1967), pp. 20-1.

23 See Freud's *An Outline of Psycho-Analysis*, p. 23.

Chapter IV

THE INSTINCTS AND THE COMPLEXES

Under psycho-analytic doctrine, the nature of a complex is to some extent dependent upon the particular instinct or instincts to which it is pertinent. For this reason, it is convenient that the two subjects of the instincts and the complexes should be treated together in the same chapter, with discussion of the instincts naturally preceding that of the complexes.

Nature of the instincts according to psycho-analysis

The word 'instinct' is what lawyers call a *nomen generalissimum,* applicable to a great variety of items and instances. So it is that anthropologists have sometimes made reference to 'group-maintaining' instincts, in which they have included parental instincts and the herd instinct, while many people still speak of an instinct of self-preservation.[1] To take an example from legal practice, it is a familiar cliché when advising against a certain opinion or certain course of action to say: 'All my instincts as a lawyer are against it'. Here, instinct is synonymous with professional intuition. In other words, in this broad sense an instinct may be developed as well as being innate, provided that it is basic to the personality.

[1] Freud himself made a number of references to the instinct of self-preservation. In 1932, he said that the instinct was 'certainly of an erotic nature', and to gain its ends, necessitated 'aggressive action'. See Exchange of Open Letters, Albert Einstein-Sigmund Freud, p. 42. In his earlier theoretical structure, Freud identified so-called 'ego-instincts', being those directed to self-preservation and to the warding-off of external dangers; but this hypothesis gave way to the more refined theory of the instincts described in this chapter.

The psycho-analytic connotation of the instincts is narrower, embracing not these cases, but the inner fundamental urges or drives of the personality contained in the id. These are primarily of two categories—the erotic or sexual, and the aggressive. The dual instinct doctrine is applied as a general working tool, although there have been refinements in the theory concerning the nature of the two basic instinctual urges or drives. It will be observed that the expressions 'urges' and 'drives' have been used, since these serve as a closer rendering of Freud's original term, *'Trieb'*. Freud distinguished three special concepts in connection with the instincts, the 'aim', 'object', and 'source'.

The aim of an instinct is to secure gratification by eliminating the associated tension; the object of an instinct is that through which the aim can be realised (e.g., a person of the opposite sex); and the source, which is not so important for psycho-analytic doctrine, is the source of stimulation within the body. An instinct operates with constancy and continuity. This is a biological characteristic,[2] and means that the instinct, as a general rule, is available for investment in objects. According to Freud, the instincts are not confined to a single area of the mind, but may be operative everywhere. Freud also conceived that the instincts involved psychic energy, and this concept of instinctual energy is fundamental in his treatment. However, as has been pointed out, 'a strictly speaking quantifying approach to these energic problems has so far not been developed.'[3]

In relation to the concept of energy, two mental processes were differentiated. First were the primary processes, involving a tendency towards the complete discharge of mental energy without delay. This is where the unconscious instinctive drive takes control, as in dreams (see Chapter VI). Secondly, there were secondary processes, where reality governs the discharge of mental energy, which discharge may therefore be delayed or controlled by the rational operation of the ego.

In its turn, the concept of psychic energy, instinctually based, leads to another concept to which Freud attached importance, namely that of 'cathexis'. Somewhat upon the analogy of an electric charge, the instinctual energy is deemed to attach itself to a mental process directed to an object, and 'cathexis' (taken from the

[2] The biological role of the instincts in keeping us alive is a point also to be stressed. See Marjorie Brierley in *International Journal of Psycho-Analysis,* Vol. 50 (1969), at pp. 451-2.

[3] Dr Heinz Hartmann in Sidney Hook (ed.), *Psychoanalysis . . .* , p. 12.

Greek word for 'occupy') denotes the total of the energy invested in such object. An object may be 'cathected', although the person from whom the cathexis derives may never have actually seen it in tangible or physical form. This may be the case even if the object, in the case of a human being, be quite unaware of the cathexis. An example is the common practice of 'pin-ups', representing male or female film and television stars. The opposite of 'cathexis', 'de-cathexis', is an instinctual urge which has been satisfied by the elimination of the tension in relation to a particular object.

The concept of psychic energy, to which Freud adhered to the last,[4] did not, from the methodological point of view, appeal to all psycho-analysts. It has recently come under attack.[5] The suggested difficulties include the following: quantification or measurement of such assumed energy is not scientifically possible; all energy in the psyche cannot be attributed to instinctual sources; there is an absence of correlation with the known energies having their source in the central nervous system. Upon one view, the whole theory should be discarded as untenable.[6] On the other hand, as a rough working hypothesis, regarding the term 'energy' as a metaphor and not as a scientifically exact expression, it does seem to be useful in elucidating the mental processes conditioned by the instincts.

In his last formulation of the theory of the instincts,[7] Freud reduced the basic instincts to two only; 'Eros', and the 'destructive instinct', corresponding to the former sexual and aggressive instincts. However, 'Eros' is much wider in range than the sexual urge, combining all that impels to self-preservation and the preservation of the species, for the purpose of 'binding together', while the destructive instinct operates in a contrary sense to destroy, to undo connections, and to reduce living things to an inorganic state. Freud called the destructive instinct the death instinct. The death instinct had first been postulated by him in 1920, and this identification of it as one the two basic instincts represented the final crystallization of Freud's thoughts on the matter (see Chapter IX). This absorption of the aggressive urge into the folds of the death

4 See his *An Outline of Psycho-Analysis,* pp. 24-5.

5 Allen D. Rosenblatt, and James T. Thickstun, 'A Study of the Concept of Psychic Energy' *International Journal of Psycho-Analysis,* Vol. 51 (1970), pp. 265-278. Cf. Adrienne Applegarth, 'Comments on Aspects of the Theory of Psychic Energy', *Journal of the American Psychoanalytic Association,* Vol. 19 (1971), pp. 379-416.

6 Rosenblatt and Thickstun, loc. cit.

7 *An Outline of Psycho-Analysis,* pp. 5-7.

instinct has not proved generally acceptable to all psycho-analysts. One point which is not clear is whether the object of the aggressive drive is invariably and in all cases to destroy.[8] For example work itself, which may be constructive, involves aggressive effort. Freud's answer would probably be that given in 1939, namely, that the two basic instincts may work against each other or blend in an alloy with each other.[9] For example, the sexual act is an act of aggression having as its purpose an intimate union, and which may result in the preservation of the species.

Psycho-analytic conception of sexuality

Misconceptions abound regarding the psycho-analytic approach towards sexuality. These range from impressions that psycho-analysis emphasizes unduly the aspect of physical sex, to the exclusion of love, to the extreme notion that it is concerned with sex and nothing else.

The truth is that psycho-analytic doctrine does not place exclusive emphasis upon the physical side of sex. Love itself is of central importance in psycho-analytic theories of human development, for the protracted, biological dependence of human beings during infancy and early adolescence conditions a need for love. Also, Freud pleaded for a wider identification between men, urging them to act upon the adage 'Love thy neighbour as thyself', as a means for countering the propensity for war.[10] Apart from this, psycho-analytic doctrine ascribes the broadest of meanings to sexuality, not confining it to the actual physical relationship of coitus. Rather, it covers the non-coital components of, and the 'energy' behind, the sexual drive. That energy is known in psycho-analytic nomenclature as the *libido*. The concept of libido may be regarded as of biological value. Sexuality covers love and sensual pleasure, including the sensual pleasures of early infancy and homosexuality as well as heterosexuality.[11]

As an illustration of the wide range of this conception of sexu-

[8] See Charles Brenner, 'The Psychoanalytic Concept of Aggression', *International Journal of Psycho-Analysis,* Vol. 52 (1971), p. 137, at pp. 139-40.

[9] See *An Outline of Psycho-Analysis,* pp. 6-7.

[10] See Exchange of Open Letters, Albert Einstein-Sigmund Freud, pp. 48-9.

[11] In a letter of 9 April 1935, Freud wrote that homosexuality 'cannot be classified as an illness' but is considered as 'a variation of the sexual function, produced by a certain arrest of sexual development'; *Letters of Sigmund Freud,* New York 1960, p. 423.

ality, it may be observed that many psycho-analysts would regard the mingling of men in clubs from which women are barred, as a manifestation to some extent of underlying homosexual wishes. It is of course fallacious to say that psycho-analysis is exclusively concerned with sex, for the aggressive drive is little less basic than the sexual.

The broad meaning of sexuality underlies the psycho-analytic theories concerning infantile sexuality, and concerning the course of sexual development of the individual. Consistently with it, sexual perversions or sexual deviances are treated as manifestations of sexuality, not as abnormal, non-sexual phenomena. Likewise, from the standpoint of psycho-analysis, sexuality is not extinguished by the advent of the menopause or the male climacteric.

Undoubtedly, psycho-analysis has emphasized the importance of sexuality and of the libidinal aspects of personality to a degree greater than in traditional psychology. For this, psycho-analysts have been derided. From experience of legal practice, and particularly in the fields of divorce, domestic relations, and criminal law, the author is unable to agree with this criticism, or with the view that undue importance has been attached by psycho-analysis to sexuality and to the libido. The healthy realism in that regard of psycho-analysis can only be commended, and has already exercised a certain beneficent influence in the legal domain.[12]

As instancing the tendency to write down the significance of sexuality in individual and social behaviour, reference may be made to the view that some tendencies and motivations in the personality are responses, by way of adaptation, to environment and circumstances, rather than conditioned by sexual impulses. The concept of adaptability is no doubt significant in human biology, and is relevant to psycho-analytical ego psychology. But it cannot be used to negate the influence of libidinal urges and processes. For example, to regard mixed dancing as merely an expression of human culture and as a method of social entertainment would be to overlook the element of libidinal pleasure involved, as well as the motives of many of the dancers. A sensual manifestation is not any the less sensual because it has been facilitated by the social and cultural milieu.

[12] Cf. the course given currently in the Harvard Law School under the title 'Psycho-analytic Theory and Legal Assumptions', which is designed to familiarise law students with the psycho-analytic theory of human behaviour, and to explore its relevance to a variety of legal issues, including those arising in the law of crimes, divorce, wills, and race relations.

Infantile sexuality; theory of sexual development

In psycho-analytic doctrine, there are some fundamental views concerning the existence of infantile sexuality, and concerning the course of sexual development from infancy to adulthood. In broad outline, the theory is as follows.

Sexual feeling begins in infancy,[13] rather than adolescence, and is then primarily related to pleasure connected with certain erotogenic parts or zones of the body.

For some not clearly determined reason, infantile sexuality comes to a standstill in the fifth or sixth year of childhood, whereupon it lies dormant until the phase of pre-puberty in the eleventh, twelfth, or thirteenth year. Then there is a renaissance of sexuality. The period of abatement of sexual feeling is known as the *latency* period.

As a general rule, infantile sexuality proceeds through a succession of stages, beginning with the oral stage associated with the experience, sensual to the child, of sucking.[14] This is followed by the anal stage, in connection with toilet training, and next by the genital stage, involving the pleasurable sensations from playing with genitals. With boys, there may be additionally the Oedipal situation of resentment against the father for monopolizing the love of the mother. With girls, there may be a similar Oedipal situation, the mother being the rival for the father's attention, and the genital stage may also involve, as claimed by psycho-analytical doctrine, feelings of penis envy and desires to emulate boys.

After the interruption of the latency period, sexuality is gradually reborn in the pre-puberty phase. Normally, there is then a revival of the genital stage, moving towards a more mature development. It is recognized that there can be complications in the pre-puberty and early puberty phases, particularly in the case of female sexuality. Regarding these, generalizations are scarcely possible.

This represents only a broad picture of infantile sexuality and sexual development according to psycho-analysis. It is recognized that there may be variations in the intensity of infantile sensual feelings; the length of time taken by each of the oral, anal, and genital stages, the Oedipal situation, and genital maturity in the phase of early puberty.

[13] General acceptance of the psycho-analytic theory as to infantile sexuality is reflected in modern books on child psychology. Cf. Sandström, *The Psychology of Childhood and Adolescence,* Pelican Edition 1968, pp. 159-60.

[14] Breast feeding, bottle feeding, finger sucking, etc.

Yet some psycho-analytical books and studies convey the impression that there is a stereotyped pattern of sexual development in and after infancy, which *every* person has undergone. This would be absurd. Frequently, the oral stage has continued into the third and fourth year of childhood, while in the case of some children the anal stage has come and gone briefly, with little or no feeling and without leaving any significant mental traces. It may perhaps be queried whether a protracted oral stage can leave room for any reasonably defined anal or genital stages.

The two central hypothesis of infantile sexuality, and of the latency period, have stood the test of time and been confirmed by data other than those which led Freud to his views on this matter.[15] Yet even today they are subject to criticism. This is perhaps partly due to a lingering misunderstanding of the psycho-analytical concept of sexuality—not realizing that it extends to sensual gratification, unconnected with sexual intercourse. Another explanation is that given by Freud himself, that infantile amnesia during the latency period of events preceding that period conceals from every person the beginnings of his own sexual life.

It must be said that the oral-anal-genital pattern does not necessarily provide a comprehensive explanation of all infantile sensual satisfactions. For example, clinical data have revealed that there may be both in male and female children an intense interest in the urethra and in urination. The penis envy theory itself reflects such an interest in the case of girls, and as Havelock Ellis thought, there may be an element of innate sexuality in urethral eroticism.

With regard to the penis envy theory, it is believed that it is formulated in too general a manner. Statements in the psycho-analytical literature insisting that all girls experience this feeling at some time or another in early childhood smack of humourless pedantry. It may be true that the majority do experience such envy during infancy, but there is a minority none the less in whom visual awareness of the penis in boys arouses no feeling of envy, no desire of emulation of the opposite sex. They may be mildly curious or apathetic or, in many cases, simply amused.

The components of sexuality

References will be found in the psycho-analytical literature to the component sexual 'instincts', covering sexual tendencies associated

[15] E.g., the data of direct child observation; cf Sandström, *The Psychology of Childhood and Adolescence*, pp. 159, and 201-2.

with certain erotogenic parts of the body, or reflecting some intensification of some mental element in sexual behaviour. The expression 'instincts', used in this connection, may give rise to misunderstandings. For example, sadism and masochism are said to represent component instincts; sadism being considered as an extension of the active role of the male in the sexual relationship, and masochism as an amplification of the passive role of the female in that relationship. But this fact does not give them the character of instincts. They remain no more than components of the sexual instinct.

Nevertheless, the psycho-analytical doctrine on the formation and status of these component tendencies of sexuality represents one of its most important contributions to the understanding of human personality. The identification of the sensual basis of personality characteristics has provided valuable psychological insights. Freud and his collaborators were certainly not the first persons in history to perceive the sexual implications of exhibitionism, sadism, masochism, and other trends in individual behaviour. But, together with pioneers such as Havelock Ellis, they were outstanding in the effort to construct a scientific body of theory, explanatory of these in the context of the whole personality. Here again, from experience in legal practice, the author is unable to agree with the criticism that psycho-analysts have unduly emphasized the sexual basis of these tendencies. Indeed with some persons, the sensual element is quite perceptible, and long cultivation of such tendencies gives them a life of their own, to which they become habituated. In this case the tendencies may almost be said to be additionally sexualized.

Sexual perversions, so-called, have been brought within the scope of the psycho-analytical doctrine regarding the development of the components of sexuality. In this doctrine, the point is well brought out that the young child is uninhibited in its sensual attachments to different parts of the body, as well as to the body's functions, and knows nothing of socially disapproved perversions.[16] Empirical data support the view that, in the case of certain persons, sexual deviances have their origin in early infancy, undergoing a process of unconscious fixation, from which point there is no advance to sexual maturity or, if there is such an advance, the tendency remains. It would seem also that conditions in the early phase of puberty, including the home environment, may operate as

[16] Freud described infants as 'polymorphously perverse'. See *A General Introduction to Psychoanalysis,* p. 186.

an additional factor to determine the question whether or not progress can be made to normality, with the fixation disappearing, for in the later years of adulthood, psycho-analytical treatment in regard to such fixations seems to have less chance of success than had it been undertaken in early adolescence. In all fairness to psycho-analysis, the criticism that it has proclaimed perversions to be beyond the reach of conscious control is unjust. Primarily, it has emphasized the difficulties involved in dethroning the unconscious fixations related to these perversions.

An intense expression in infancy of a particular sensual tendency may lead to a strong fixation, but this does not explain all cases of powerful fixations. One theory which may explain some special instances is that the fixation has acquired its force through the child's retreat, out of fear or of conflict, from the genital stage of infantile sexual development. However, as the clinical data indicate, there are numerous possibilities of variation in the circumstances giving rise to an infantile sensual fixation, which fails to give way when adulthood is reached.[17]

The characterization of such a fixation as a perversion or sexual deviance is a value-judgment dictated by the *mores* of our current Western society and culture. It is possible to conceive of societies and cultures in which a particular perversion or deviance, now repugnant to such *mores,* would be considered unobjectionable, and perhaps as normal. Therefore, the expression 'fixation' is a relative one, conditioned not by absolute values of personality development but by socio-cultural standards.

One of Freud's major propositions concerning the components of the sexual instinct was what he called their 'plasticity'—the ease with which they can change their aims or undergo displacement from one object to another, and with which one form of gratification can be substituted for another. Moreover, gratification can be delayed or suspended or repressed or inhibited or even undergo transformation. To some extent, this applies also to the aggressive instinct. Biologically speaking, this is a significant feature of human psychology. To quote a distinguished psycho-analyst: 'The lesser rigidity of the human drives, the comparatively easy shift of the aims, the freeing of many activities from a rigid connection with one definite instinctual tendency, the comparative independence from and variety of possible responses to outer and inner

17 One theory is that some perversions may be due to early disturbances in the relationship between the mother and the infant. See Phyllis Greenacre in *Psychoanalytic Study of the Child,* Vol. XXIII (1968), p. 57.

stimuli have to be taken into account in considering the role of the drives in human psychology'.[18]

This 'plasticity' of the instincts explains the mental processes of 'displacement', that is, the transference of an emotional attitude from one idea or person to another; of 'projection', the attribution to another person of an attitude, wish, or tendency felt to be repugnant; and of 'regression', that return to an earlier, usually infantile phase of a person's instinctual development, or to an earlier fixation. Moreover, so far as the sexual instinct is concerned, mental processes and attitudes can become 'sexualized', in the sense of giving the person concerned a sensual satisfaction in adopting them. Even anxiety itself may become sexualized (see Chapter V).

The instinct of aggression

While the aggressive instinct is innate, and in a sense independent, it can nevertheless ally itself in a number of ways with the sexual instinct. In the first place, there is an element of aggressivity in the role of the male in the sexual relationship. Secondly, in sadism and masochism, aggressivity is fused with the sensual tendencies of inflicting and receiving pain, being directed outward in the former case and inward in the latter.

On the other hand, where the aggressive impulses become intensified through some special cause, the effect in the generality of instances is temporarily to suspend or diminish sexuality. It is said that a sick man makes a poor lover, but it is equally true that a man occupied with revenge, or another predominantly aggressive urge makes a poor lover, or no lover at all. This is consistent with Freud's view that the two instincts seldom appear in isolation. As he has said, the aggressive instinct is '*always* alloyed' with the erotic instinct.

A further illustration of the close connection between sexuality and aggression is what occurs, in some cases, where an individual has repressed homosexual wishes. A person with such wishes will project his inner aggression, corresponding to his inner repugnance to homosexuality, upon another person who has, or who is assumed to have homosexual tendencies, and will react aggressively towards the latter.

Moreover, if an excess of aggressivity can operate to reduce the

[18] Dr Heinz Hartmann in Sidney Hook (ed.), *Psychoanalysis* . . . , p. 11.

sexual drive, it is correlatively true that normal aggressivity can be diminished by gratification of the sexual instinct.

The ability of the aggressive instinct to shift and move is parallel with that of the sexual instinct.[19] Aggressivity can be displaced to another object, or again, through the mechanism of projection, a person may find his own aggressive feelings replaced by the impression that some other person is behaving aggressively towards him.

The relationship between aggressivity and the postulated death instinct, according to Freud, is discussed in Chapter IX.

The importance that psycho-analysis attaches to aggression is not generally appreciated, partly because there is a widespread impression that psycho-analysts give undue or exclusive emphasis to sexuality. As indicated in Chapter III, the super-ego may be considered as an alloy of several mental processes, including the internalization of aggression, and indeed the unconscious nature of aggressive impulses and wishes is one of the most serious difficulties requiring to be surmounted in psycho-analytical treatment. Not only may it take some considerable time to make a patient aware of unconscious aggressivity, but there still remains the problem of rational control of free-floating, undirected aggressive drives. At the conclusion of therapy, the patient must stand on his own feet, and empirically learn how to channel into useful directions, in harmony with his social environment, that excess of aggressivity which cannot be neutralized through libidinal satisfactions or otherwise.

The complexes

A complex may be defined as a group of attitudes and tendencies of a person, linked together because of a common unconscious origin, and having a common emotional character. The word 'complex' is now a commonplace of our language. It must be admitted that the expression did not originate with Freud; he expressly acknowledge that, in using it, he was indebted to the Zurich school of psychiatrists (Bleuler, Jung and others).[20]

Undoubtedly, the two best-known complexes, in a popular sense, are the inferiority complex and the persecution complex. In psycho-analytical theory, on the other hand, the two most important complexes are the castration complex and the Oedipus complex.

19 Yet it is believed that the aggressive urge is more rigid and less plastic, in its displaceability, than the sexual drive. See J. Lampl-de Groot in *International Journal of Psycho-Analysis,* Vol. 50 (1969), p. 567.

20 Freud's first use of the expression appears to have been in the 1907 edition of *The Psychopathology of Everyday Life,* originally published in 1901.

The castration complex

The castration complex is said to affect a great many persons, in varying degrees of intensity, and to lie at the root of some of the more severe forms of neurosis. It is believed by certain psycho-analysts to be an almost universal affliction of mankind. Yet it cannot be described as only of clinical significance, for it may manifest itself in tendencies and personality characteristics which do not impair the capacity of the individual to cope with life.

The psycho-analytical doctrine regarding the origins of the castration complex, and the manner in which that complex continues as part of the unconscious to influence human behaviour, has been attacked as highly conjectural and based upon data derived from the examination of patients suffering from grave nervous disorders. Yet there is much material in the descriptive anthropological literature to support that doctrine.

In men, the castration complex is conceived as having its source at the time when the boy is conscious of, or playing with his genitals. One or other of the parents, or a parent-figure may threaten loss or injury to an important part of the child's body, sometimes even naming the penis, or this may be hinted at or inferred. The object is to stop the boy playing with his genitals, or to put an end to some other form of misbehaviour.[21] Indeed, there may not be even the semblance of a hint or inference of a threat.

The fear of castration may overwhelm the child on account of circumcision of a baby brother, or through sight of the female genitals. Hence, it is believed by some psycho-analysts that there is some inherited, primeval characteristic of the unconscious which facilitates the onset of the castration fear, and accentuates its intensity and poignancy. Otherwise, the situation would have been of only transient importance, without leaving a mental trace.

The assumed fear of castration can also arise in the boy's fantasies in the course of the Oedipal situation when, according to psycho-analytical theory, he may come to fear retaliation by the father for death wishes, and for the desire to monopolize the love of the mother.

Yet how does the castration complex come to be embedded in the unconscious? The point may be academic, but a multiplicity of explanations can be offered, probably because the circumstances giving rise to the complex can vary so much. Possible theories include the following: the castration fear may become fused with

21 E.g., repeated bed-wetting.

the process of introjection of the super-ego, i.e. the internalization of parental authority as described in the previous chapter; the child may react to an assumed fear of castration with aggressivity directed against the parents, and as this is not in harmony with his love for his parents, the fear and the aggressive impulses, linked together, may be subject to repression; the experience giving rise to the castration fear may be traumatic, and like some other severe emotional experiences in early infancy disappear into the unconscious with the supervention of the latency period; or, if the fear of castration arose out of an assumed threat for playing with his genitals, since the fear was connected with conduct known to be prohibited by parental authority, both the fear and the situation producing it may, through repression, be banished to the unconscious. It is emphasized that the threat may be taken as one of injury to the genitals, and not solely as loss of the phallus.

The existence of a castration complex, as postulated by psycho-analytical doctrine, is supported not only by the data mentioned above, but in the case of certain persons by the presence of a deep fear, conscious or unconscious, of undergoing loss of virility, or by sexual impotence, psychically due to unconscious or sometimes conscious dread of injury to the phallus through intercourse. Dream material provides further confirmation. But perhaps the best proof of the complex is the extent to which it underlies a widespread type of anxiety neurosis.

In the case of women, there is, according to psycho-analytical theory, nothing exactly equivalent. For one thing, there can be no fear of future castration in the little girl. However the analysis of some women has revealed the existence of infantile fantasies of earlier possession of the phallus and its loss through castration. In some of these cases there is a wish to be compensated for the assumed loss by the bearing of a child. As will be seen, the special nature of this female castration complex plays an important role in determining both the commencement and the nature of the Oedipal phase experienced by girls. Whereas in the case of boys it is the Oedipal situation which may give rise to the castration complex, it is the latter complex which paves the way for the Oedipal phase of girls.

Oedipus complex

Some Oedipal situations may be of a complicated nature, as clinical case-material shows. Freud persuasively drew a distinction between the simple straightforward complex and what he referred to as a more complete Oedipus complex. In the straight-out category of Oedipus complex, there is the familiar combination of an ambivalent[22] love-hate relationship towards the father, and of a desire to monopolize the mother's love. In the more complete Oedipus complex, the bisexual character of boys comes into account. Hence the more complete Oedipus complex is characterized by an ambivalent love-hate attitude towards the father, an affectionate relationship with the mother, and at the same time an affectionate, passive-feminine attitude towards the father with some corresponding hostility towards the mother. Freud's view should not be taken as a universally applicable generalization, but it is certainly explanatory of a number of special cases of boys with perceptible feminine tendencies.

It is a matter of controversy whether or not the Oedipus complex only affects persons who are members of a Western-type, family-culture society.[23] Anthropological evidence, including the data contained in the literature of descriptive anthropology, is inconclusive. It may be said, however, that although the Oedipus complex may not be a universal psychological phenomenon, there is at least a universal susceptibility to be affected by such a complex if the appropriate conditions and environment so allow. This is reflected in the fact that in some communities in under-developed countries, observers have identified an Oedipus-type rivalry in children, with aggressive impulses directed not against the parents, but against parent-substitutes such as uncles and brothers.[24] The existence of some sort of family culture would seem to be the *sine qua non* for a child to become subject to an Oedipus or Oedipus-type complex.

A major theoretical problem of psycho-analysis is to explain the rather different course of development of the Oedipus complex in girls. Freud's view was that the difference corresponded essentially to a difference in the reaction to the implied suggestion of castra-

22 A word first coined by Bleuler in 1910 to denote the co-existence in one person of antithetic emotional attitudes; e.g. love and hate.

23 Note in this connection Professor Arlow's reference to the Oedipal phase as 'a regular developmental phase to be observed in children reared in family patterns in civilized society'. See Sidney Hook (ed.), *Psychoanalysis . . .* , pp. 208-9.

24 See M.-C. and E. Ortigues, *Oedipe Africain,* Paris, 1968; A. Kardiner and R. Linton, *The Individual and His Society,* New York 1939, pp. 384-9; A. Kardiner, with others, *The Psychological Frontiers of Society,* New York 1945, pp. 353-4; *Letters of Sigmund Freud,* p. 432 (Freud's speculation that Napoleon was impelled by Oedipal rivalry for his elder brother, Joseph, filling the place of a father in the family culture in Corsica at that time).

tion. In the case of boys, the Oedipus complex prepares the ground for the castration complex, with the result that under the threat of castration the Oedipus complex is supplanted, by being repressed or abandoned, sometimes leaving a severe super-ego behind it. In the case of girls, however, it is the castration complex which prepares the way for the Oedipal situation, instead of supplanting it. The assumed castration and accompanying wish for compensation brings the girl, who was formerly attached to her mother, closer to her father, with some aggressivity directed against the mother. In time the castration fear vanishes, and the girl's feminity is encouraged so that the Oedipus complex, far from being repressed or abandoned, has a tendency to continue.[25]

It is considered useful to distinguish the Oedipus complex and the Oedipal phase.[26] The Oedipal phase refers to that period in childhood, during which the Oedipus complex generates the various reactions characteristic of it, a curious blend of sexual and aggressive feelings about the parents. When the Oedipal phase is terminated, the legacy of the Oedipus complex remains in the unconscious, and may condition adult attitudes, wishes and behaviour throughout life.

The inferiority and persecution complexes

We can deal only briefly with the inferiority complex and the persecution complex. These are the most perceptible complexes in everyone's experience, while in the case of the inferiority complex, the person concerned is himself usually conscious of his affliction. However, the individual with a persecution complex is seldom conscious that he has it, though this may be quite obvious to others. There may be unconscious factors operating in both cases.[27]

Sometimes it is the unconscious castration complex, manifesting itself in an underlying fear of loss of virility, that may condition the inferiority complex in a particular person. In other instances, the inferiority complex is due to a low degree of narcissism, or to the operation of masochistic tendencies, with the aggressive instinct directed inward against the self.

[25] Cf. study by J. Lampl-de Groot, 'The Evolution of the Oedipus Complex in Women' (1927) in Robert Fliess (ed.), *The Psycho-Analytic Reader*, London 1950, pp. 180-94.

[26] Cf. Professor Arlow in Sidney Hook (ed.), *Psychoanalysis* . . . , p. 208.

[27] There can of course be other explanations. A succession of failures can produce an inferiority complex, while a persecution complex is known to be a symptom in some cases of heart disease.

The persecution complex, or paranoid attitude, may manifest itself in a mild or in a pathological form. Sometimes, it can be explained as the repetition in adulthood of an emotional pattern of childhood, when there may have occurred a feeling of rejection by, or lack of love on the part of parents and parent-figures. In the more pathological cases, psycho-analysts have been able to detect unconscious homosexual attitudes, which call into play strong reaction-formations of an aggressive character against persons with whom relations would be naturally on a normal friendly level.

Simple as they may appear on the surface, both complexes can be the expression of very involved unconscious forces.

Chapter V

GUILT AND ANXIETY

The sense or consciousness of guilt and the condition of neurotic anxiety are two emotional states which, either as causes or as effects or responses, can exert influence over large areas of the mental life of the persons so affected. Psycho-analysis has made an important contribution towards clarification of the nature and origins of guilt and anxiety, and in respect to the therapeutic aspects, although it cannot yet be said to have produced a fully comprehensive theory as to both conditions. For this reason, it is still customary to speak of the 'problem of guilt' and the 'problem of anxiety', phrases which suggest the element of insolubility.

In the matter of therapy, both conditions can show varying degrees of intractability. It is fair to say that mitigation or alleviation is more common than complete cure, while some acute cases are particularly resistant to psycho-analytic therapy.

If this were not enough, the position is also that there are different kinds and degrees of the sense of guilt, and different kinds and degrees of anxiety states. But one generalization is possible: apart from instances of anxiety caused by frustration, neurotic guilt and anxiety conditions represent a re-animation of infantile conflicts and dilemmas. To a large extent, the acuteness of the condition—for guilt and anxiety to a non-pathological level are experienced normally by a considerable portion of the population in present-day communities—is due to some absence of tolerance in the particular individual affected by it. Mainly because of the infantile origins of both conditions, they are treated together in the present chapter.

Relationship between guilt and anxiety

A sense of guilt can occur without the person concerned experiencing an anxiety state, and equally there may be an anxiety state, independent of any sense of guilt. Thus, a person can have a feeling of guilt through having failed to achieve an ambition coinciding with his ego-ideal, but this may fall short of neurotic anxiety. As an illustration of the converse case, anxiety can be experienced through the inability to release strong aggressive impulses which are not repressed without the existence of any feeling of guilt.

It is true also that a neurotic person may have symptoms expressly designed to prevent the suffering of anxiety, as in the case of phobias and obsessional practices: the express purpose is to ward off anxiety. This is not quite the same with feelings of guilt. There is less dread of guilt than of anxiety, although a person may seek to conduct himself in order to avoid experiencing guilt. On the other hand, guilt feelings can escalate into hysterical or semi-hysterical anxiety. At the same time, the basis of an anxiety state is often an unconscious sense of guilt. As Freud pointed out, the person concerned does not feel guilty but only ill, with his muted sense of guilt not conveying any conscious feeling of being guilty. So we are forced to admit that in many cases there is no sharp division between guilt and anxiety.

In complicated neuroses, guilt and anxiety can co-exist, and in a variety of combinations. For example, a person may be susceptible to a number of anxiety conditions, some of which are independent of a sense of guilt which he consciously feels, while other anxiety conditions are an expression of an unconscious sense of guilt. Moreover, if guilt can nourish anxiety, it seems equally true that anxiety can reinforce guilt. The inability to tolerate or cope with anxiety states may be felt as a self-depreciatory lapse from the ego-ideal.

Nature and origins of sense of guilt

Psycho-analytic doctrine provides a cogent explanation of the nature and origin of the sense of guilt felt by an adult person, irrespective of whether this is or is not a neurotic state. One point is well made, namely that a sense of guilt does not date only from the formation of the super-ego. Even before the process of internalization of parental authority begins which leads to the establishment of the super-ego, a child may consciously experience a sense of guilt through misbehaviour against the wishes of parents or parent-figures. Thus, it is felt originally as a fear of authority, coupled with the tension associated with the thought that there may be loss of love from, or punishment by the displeased parent.

As for the sense of guilt felt *after* the formation of the super-ego, this according to psycho-analytic doctrine corresponds to a perception in the ego of the disapproval of the super-ego; an assessment by the ego of the tensions between its own strivings and the demands of the super-ego. Thus, at bottom, it is a reproduction of the childish fear of authority felt in infancy after misbehaviour condemned by the parents or parent-figures. It will be observed that this theory makes the ego the seat of the feeling of guilt. But there may be an unconscious sense of guilt, which is experienced as anxiety or as tension only, but not as a conscious feeling of guilt. For instance, unconscious homosexual wishes may be condemned by the super-ego, leading to unconscious guilt.

Psycho-analysis has made it clear that both normal and neurotic persons may carry around an unconscious load of guilt, without being guilty of any actual wrongdoing in adulthood, and this may lead them in some instances either to commit crimes in order to rid themselves of the unconscious tension, or for similar reasons to accept liability for crimes never committed.[1] Psycho-analysts maintain that the primary focus of unconscious guilt is the Oedipal situation of early childhood, with its death wishes against the father and sensual love of the mother now banished to the unconscious. The classical Oedipal situation may not have occurred as a fact, but clinical data taken as a whole support the view that infantile relationships with the parents lie at the root of an unconscious sense of guilt in most cases.

Freud has cogently explained why the subsisting, buried and forbidden wish can remain as a permanent source of unconscious guilt: it cannot be concealed from the super-ego, and the conflict with the inner voice of conscience maintains the tension expressed in the sense of guilt. In a similar situation in the period of infancy, the conflict is external, with the child facing a threat of punishment by, or loss of love from the authoritarian parent.

[1] See the interesting judgment of Chief Judge Bazelon, dealing with this point, in the case of *Miller v. United States* (1963), 320 F. 2d. 767. In a seminar address in 1906, entitled 'Psycho-Analysis and the Ascertaining of Truth in Courts of Law' Freud warned judges that an accused person might appear guilty of the precise charge laid against him, although actually innocent of it, because he was guilty of some other act or offence with which he was not charged; *Collected Papers*, Vol. II, London 1924, p. 13, at p. 23.

Guilt comes into play in three forms of mental and neurotic disorder: melancholia;[2] obsessional neurosis; and hysteria. In melancholia and obsessional neurosis, the central feature is generally the over-intensity of the sense of guilt, which is dominantly conscious in melancholia. How this degree of intensity supervenes is not fully explained in psycho-analytical theory, nor why there should be the sudden onset of the disorder after years during which the sense of guilt has lain dormant without erupting pathologically. In hysteria, one feature is that the ego is constantly avoiding perception of the criticisms of the super-ego. But here again it is not fully explained why the disorder should suddenly break out in adulthood. If psycho-analytical doctrine were consistent on this point, it would have to be admitted that some children are of hysterical disposition and the future victims of adult hysteria. This may be correct, but how is this condition to be detected by parents before adolescence begins?

There is some controversy among psycho-analysts regarding the precise difference between guilt and shame, although it seems generally admitted that shame is usually a form of self-depreciation which may or may not be associated with guilt, and is fairly easily identifiable. Thus a person may feel ashamed of the fact that he is driving an old model car or of the social origins of his parents, but this need not involve any feeling of guilt, although it may in the case of an individual with a sensitive conscience.

The sense of guilt attains pathological shape if it is associated with an unconscious need for punishment. According to some psycho-analysts, this need for punishment may be an unconscious part of the super-ego. Where it is present in patients, it constitutes a formidable obstacle to recovery, because the neurotic illness itself is deemed to be the sought after punishment, and there is a tendency to cling to the illness which fulfils the unconscious need. Thus, there is no will to recover, although consciously the patient may be seeking a cure. Methods of varying degrees of effectiveness have been adopted in order to neutralize this unconscious need for punishment. It is the constancy of this need that predominantly stands in the way of therapy.

It is apparent, then, that the sense of guilt may take quite a number of forms, and possess different degrees of intensity, while co-existing with other emotional states.

While there may not be necessarily a need for punishment, often

[2] Now called also endogenous depressive psychosis; it may sometimes be the effect of some organic illness.

there is a desire for atonement or forgiveness. This is where religion can play such an important role, and one which in itself appears to prove amply the psycho-analytical proposition of the widespread presence in normal people of an unconscious sense of guilt. The minister or priest represents a parent-figure, and in a sense a re-externalization of the conscience of the worshippers who look to him for guidance. There is a regression to the infantile condition where parental authority was so decisive; and by his forgiveness, the minister or priest can temporarily relieve a worshipper of his sense of guilt. But this religious process must be a long one if it is to be effective in allaying guilt. Of itself, it does not result in any effective reduction of the severity of the super-ego. Psychiatric techniques, of which psycho-analytical therapy is one, are necessary if the super-ego is to undergo any permanent alteration in its strictness and rigidity.

The difficulties of therapy in ministering to a sense of guilt, both as regards the strengthening of the ego and as regards converting a stern super-ego into one less unrelenting, are not however to be minimized.

Psycho-analytic doctrine relating to neurotic anxiety

Neurotic anxiety may be not only itself a disorder, but also a key factor in a number of neuroses. Professor Robert Waelder well described neurotic anxiety as 'anxiety in situations in which average people can either detect no danger at all or no danger great enough to justify the intensity of the worry'.[3] He added: 'The person who is afraid of dogs, the adult woman who is afraid to walk down Park Avenue or Regent Street in broad daylight, during the hours of heavy traffic, or the healthy young man who lives in constant terror lest he may come down with, or may already suffer from, a fatal disease, are cases in point; we then speak of neurotic anxiety because of its intensity, its refractoriness to ordinary explanations of fact and probability, and its omnipresence.' Neurotic anxiety is an emotional condition which normal persons find difficult to understand.

As in the case of the sense of guilt, neurotic anxiety can assume many forms and have degrees of intensity. This is perhaps one reason among others why it is difficult to construct a comprehensive, systematic theory to embrace all of its manifestations.

[3] See his article, 'Inhibitions, Symptoms and Anxiety: Forty Years Later', *The Psychoanalytic Quarterly*, Vol. XXXVI (1967), pp. 21-2.

There is a widespread impression that the definitive statement of psycho-analytical doctrine regarding anxiety is to be found in Freud's classical book, *Inhibitions, Symptoms and Anxiety,* published in 1926. This not entirely correct, as psycho-analytic doctrine has to some extent moved forward since then, for example, in tracing the roots of some anxiety conditions to disturbances in the earliest relationships of mother and infant. Moreover, the search for a unified theory of anxiety has continued.[4] Yet it is still necessary to remind ourselves of Freud's position in respect to anxiety, as stated in the 1926 book.[5]

Formerly, Freud had taken the view that the sexual-somatic factor was the determining factor in the outbreak of anxiety, and that the symptoms of anxiety resulted from a person's sexual habits. This led to a damming-up of sexual tensions. There was an onset of anxiety where there was insufficient discharge of the tension. The general remedy, although not the exclusive one, was a change of sexual practices.

In 1926 Freud made a radical revision of his earlier theory. The ego was now made the seat of anxiety. Neurotic anxiety was conceived as a reaction to danger in the same way as real anxiety, but the danger, instead of being external, was located in the instincts. An instinctual danger was assimilated to an objective danger. Thus instead of the transformation of the inner mental material into anxiety according to the earlier theory, it was the fear by the ego of the inner danger that constituted neurotic anxiety. To take some illustrations, under the older view, repressed or dammed up homosexual wishes or similarly frustrated aggressive wishes, unless gratified, were converted into anxiety. According to Freud's revised views, the ego was conceived to be the seat of fear of these repressed wishes.[6] Under appropriate conditions, where an object was presented for the satisfaction of the wishes, the always present fear could mount to anxiety.[7]

This was an immense step forward, both in theory and therapy.

4 See, e.g., Leo Rangell, 'A Further Attempt to Resolve the Problem of Anxiety', *Journal of the American Psychoanalytic Association,* Vol. 16 (1968), pp. 371-404 (bibliography at pp. 402-4).

5 For a discussion of the present state of psycho-analytical doctrine as to anxiety, see R. Waelder, 'Inhibitions, Symptoms and Anxiety: Forty Years Later', pp. 1-36, and his book, *Basic Theory of Psychoanalysis,* New York 1960, pp. 154-66.

6 The warning-signal of anxiety is received by the ego; see Chapter III.

7 Anxiety due to repressed aggressive wishes can be diminished by reduction of the fear of aggressivity; cf. Marjorie Brierley in *International Journal of Psycho-Analysis,* Vol. 50 (1969), pp. 451-2.

Professor Waelder has well said: 'It is not too much to say that this revision has greatly altered and enriched psycho-analytic treatment; of all the later additions to the original theory conceived at the turn of the century—additions which include narcissism, repetition compulsion, an instinct of aggression, and unconscious guilt feelings—it is perhaps the most important one'.[8]

Yet Freud appears to have retained the possible view that frustrated high-degree sexual tension, without outlet, might still be converted into anxiety under appropriate circumstances. His retention of this category has continued to be criticized, and it would seem that the reaction-to-danger theory is now largely preferred as explaining this special case. Perhaps, the truth lies between Freud's view and the modern approach. The ego may be the seat of a reaction by fear to the presence of sexual excitement, but the somatic factor seems to play some role in accentuating anxiety; a partial gratification of the tension can diminish the degree of anxiety.

Leaving this category aside, anxiety may be due to other causes, including among them: (a) fear of a severe super-ego; (b) unconscious fear of castration (see preceding chapter); and (c) fear of loss of love, expressed in an unconscious wish to be mothered, although adulthood has been attained. The first and second fears can be held by the same person, the unconsciously feared punishment to be meted out by the super-ego being that of possible castration.

In 1930, a new concept involving the 'sexualization' of anxiety was propounded by Laforgue.[9] It has now gained wide acceptance. First sensations of anxiety, whether real or neurotic, may become attached to the unconscious masochism of the person concerned, and later be reproduced repeatedly, irrespective of a reaction-to-danger situation, as gratifications of masochistic sensuality. Anxiety can, so to speak, be manufactured at the drop of a hat; the tendency may also be allied with a hysterical unconscious desire to draw attention to oneself. An inner pleasure is obtained from the repeated anxiety attacks, so that it is not incorrect to speak of an 'eroticization' of anxiety. Patients cannot easily be made conscious of this desire to obtain sensual gratification from anxiety. It is believed that such masochistic anxiety may be diminished through an increase in the subject's narcissistic self-esteem.

[8] 'Inhibitions, Symptoms and Anxiety: Forty Years Later', p. 22.

[9] See R. Laforgue, 'On the Erotization of Anxiety', *International Journal of Psycho-Analysis,* Vol. 11 (1930), pp. 312-21.

As mentioned earlier, anxiety can be the key factor in certain neuroses. These are the neuroses, the central symptom of which is the person's wish to avoid suffering anxiety; e.g., the various phobias, and obsessional practices. Thus the claustrophobic is stricken with panic if obliged to be in a closed space, and the obsessional neurotic will suffer severe anxiety if unable to perform some sacerdotal series of meaningless acts. In their ultimate long-term effects, the phobias and obsessional practices involve a serious curtailment of the ego. They are dictated sometimes by unconscious wishes, and sometimes are an expression of an unconscious sense of guilt. Where the phobia or obsessional practice has become an established ingredient of the personality, the anxiety experienced in the event of the phobia situation (e.g. closed space) not being avoided, or the obsessional ritual not being performed, is almost a semi-reflex, automatic sensation. Hence, after a phobia or obsessional practice is a conditioned part of the psyche, it seems difficult to treat its characteristic anxiety state as covered by the reaction-to-danger theory now generally adopted in psycho-analytical doctrine, although when the anxiety was initially experienced before the phobia or obsessional practice set in, it may have been within the theory. For example, the initial anxiety of the agoraphobic was a reaction in the ego, represented by fear of unconscious sexual wishes.

The author finds it difficult to integrate with psycho-analytical doctrine the cases within his experience in legal practice of anxiety states and anxiety neuroses, which have followed injuries suffered or shocks received in motor vehicle and industrial accidents. In most instances, the persons afflicted had previously been quite normal persons, devoid of neurotic symptoms. The theory may be ventured, upon the basis of long observation, that the anxiety in these cases was an expression of a desire, sometimes conscious, sometimes unconscious, to retreat from reality as though the person's psyche was helpless[10] before a situation which it found devastating, such as serious physical impairment and permanent loss of the enjoyment of life, coupled often with grave financial embarrassment.

10 This would be somewhat similar to Robert Waelder's construction of Freud's earlier theories concerning anxiety, namely that the danger giving rise to anxiety is 'everything which allows the stimulus-tensions to increase to such a degree that the psychical apparatus no longer feels able to cope with them'. See *The Psychoanalytic Quarterly*, Vol. XXXVI, (1967), p. 6.

If there is anything then which is common to these cases, and to the types of neurotic anxiety most generally dealt with in psycho-analytical doctrine and therapy, it would seem to be this characteristic of a feeling of helplessness in the ego. So, in a case of fear of instinctual danger, it may be said that the ego feels, to some extent, helplessly unable to cope with unconscious instinctual wishes.

With the intuition of the novelist and dramatist, Charles Morgan hinted at this element of helplessness in anxiety when he made reference to 'that profound anxiety, that sense of being enclosed by the irrational, the unnatural, the uncontrollable, which is the source of contemporary despairs'.[11] This is a hypothesis which is merely tentative, and may be only a partial explanation.

Some special problems raised by neurotic anxiety

The special character of acuteness of anxiety symptoms is a question that has puzzled psycho-analysts. According to one view, widely accepted, the intensity of the symptoms confirms the fact that an attack of anxiety is in effect a psychic reproduction of the trauma of birth suffered by the person concerned when a baby. This is not necessarily so with 'sexualized' anxiety, which has a kind of 'thrill' quality.

No adequate explanation is to be found in psycho-analytical doctrine for the cases where there is a first onset of anxiety, almost out of the blue, without prior experience of any similar state by the person suffering the attack. For instance, why did an adult agoraphobic have no anxiety in open spaces prior to the first attack of agoraphobic panic? It is thought by some that somatic aspects may be involved, while others believe that the first onset may have occurred through the building up of other psychic pressures and tensions, adding to the unconscious force to which the ego reacts with anxiety.[12]

Another matter calling for explanation is that of the wide variations among persons so far as the factor of anxiety-tolerance is concerned. There is no doubt that certain individuals can stand a high degree of anxiety without complaint and without producing

11 Charles Morgan, *The Writer and his World*, London 1960, p. 75. The confrontation of the psyche with a situation that is felt beyond it, may also explain to some extent the accentuation in the early phase of the male climacteric, although there are as well somatic factors involved.

12 Among other explanations offered by Freud were the theory of some special frustration, and the suggestion of an increase of the quantity of libido, upsetting the balance of health.

other neuroses such as the phobias and obsessional practices. On the other hand, phobias and obsessional practices would not exist if the persons afflicted by them had been prepared to suffer the anxiety symptoms on all occasions, come what may. We may be forced to admit that the concept adopted by followers of Pavlov, of the weak nervous system and its vulnerability in certain persons, may apply to some instances of lack of anxiety-tolerance.

Lastly, there is the fact that, according to the character and capacity of the person concerned, anxiety may so to speak be drained away by some activity before it becomes a symptom felt by the ego. Among the solvents of anxiety are such spheres of action as artistic creation, literary effort, and—for certain persons—such a mundane activity as the driving of a motor vehicle. Some of these solvents fall within the general theory of sublimation, which is dealt with in a later chapter.[13]

13 See Chapter X.

Chapter VI

SYMPTOMS AND DREAMS

According to psycho-analytic doctrine, symptoms and dreams arise as a result of the same dynamic mental processes. In both instances, there is a contest between unconscious repressed urges seeking gratification or fulfilment and conflicting forces warding them off, blocking complete satisfaction, and compelling what can only be described in metaphorical language as a compromise. Otherwise the conflict would leave no traces such as symptoms or dreams. This resulting compromise is called a *compromise-formation.* Thus symptoms and dreams belong to this same category of compromise-formations manufactured by the unconscious part of the psyche. Inasmuch as healthy persons have been found subject to dreams which, on applying analytical methods, are shown to possess this character of a compromise-formation, it is apparent that the mental dynamics are the same for non-neurotic human beings as for those suffering from neurotic disorders. This fundamental proposition, at one time considered to be radical, is now a commonplace of modern psychology and philosophy. One may find earlier hints of it in the intuitive writings of philosophers and poets, before Freud laid the foundations of psycho-analytical theory.

Freud was inclined towards a somewhat wider generalization, namely that the borderline between mental normality and neurotic disorder is of a fluid nature in all cases. He did not mean by this that the healthy condition of normal persons could in all instances be easily convertible into neurotic illness, but that, had circumstances been different — particularly the events and relationships towards the parents in infancy—a presently normal person could conceivably have become subject to a neurotic affliction.

Symptoms have also this in common with dreams that they involve a certain deflection of mental energy which is thought to come from the reservoir of the id.

Nature of a symptom; distinction from an inhibition

For behavioural philosophers, the expression 'symptom' has a wide range. They would perceive no difficulty in regarding a person's inhibition in respect to the performance of a certain act as a symptom also of that person's behavioural pattern. In common parlance, also, a pathological inhibition might be called a symptom.

This is not so in psycho-analytic doctrine, and Freud himself was careful in his classical work, *Inhibitions, Symptoms and Anxiety* (1926), to mark out the respective areas of a symptom and of an inhibition. Over forty years have passed, and apart from extensions, refinements, and illustrations of his central propositions, Freud's main ideas in this connection have, to quote Robert Waelder 'been quietly accepted and become noncontroversial parts of the clinical theory of psychoanalysis'.[1]

A symptom is primarily the effect of mental processes, and is observable by others, or perceived by the person afflicted with the symptom. An inhibition, however, is not in psycho-analytical terms the effect of a process, but a process itself, which operates in the ego. We can perhaps best illustrate this by the case of agoraphobia; on the one hand, the agoraphobic suffers from his phobic fear of open spaces, which was first manifested in an attack of anxiety, and this fear may be regarded as a true symptom, while, on the other hand, a process of restriction has taken place in his ego, precluding him from being in open spaces, and this is to be treated as an inhibition. It is characteristic of the difference between behavioural philosophers and psycho-analysts that in all probability the former would be more inclined to characterize the phobic fear as the inhibition, and the self-imposed interdiction of going to open spaces as the symptom.

Freud's hypothesis was that the inhibitions fell into three classes corresponding each to one of three categories of inhibitory processes. First, an activity may assume forbidden sexual significance, i.e. it may have an effect on a person's conscious or unconscious sexual wishes to the extent that the ego reacts by abstention from the activity. (On the conscious side, there are persons who see something repugnantly sexual in dancing and mixed bathing, while an illustration of recoil from unconscious sexual wishes is, according to psycho-analytical theory, the fear of open spaces by agoraphobics.) Second, out of a need of self-torture or self-punishment, a

[1] See his article 'Inhibitions, Symptoms and Anxiety: Forty Years Later', p. 1, at p. 35.

person may deny himself a particular activity. The self-punishment may be conscious, e.g. as in certain kinds of long fasting undertaken by individuals, or it may be of unconscious origin. Thirdly, there may be a weakening of the ego through mourning, or self-pity on account of failure, or following a long illness. The ego is then restricted and enfeebled when confronted with normal responsibilities. There is thus in all three categories a curtailment of the ego's capacity to discharge active functions.

Valid as these three categories may be for clinical purposes, they do not cover 'inhibitions' in the wider, more popular sense of the term as used in the behavioural sciences.[2] A person may often be described as having inhibitions from following a certain course of action, because of moral, ethical, or rational considerations. Nor do the categories embrace that person usually described as 'inhibited', because of natural shyness, or who is disinclined to be gregarious and to mix well in social intercourse.

Primary and secondary gains of symptoms

In psycho-analytical doctrine, a useful distinction is drawn between the primary and secondary gains of symptoms. The concept of primary gain rests upon the view that a symptom, strangely, gives some satisfaction to the afflicted individual, taking the expression 'satisfaction' in a wide and not purely subjective sense. Thus, some symptoms are substitutes for an instinctual satisfaction which is otherwise denied to the person concerned; for example, anxiety due to repressed homosexual wishes. Indeed, where anxiety is an expression of an unconscious sense of guilt, it is legitimate to say that the person suffering anxiety is nevertheless obtaining, through his symptoms, some relief from the unconscious burden.

A secondary gain is where the individual afflicted with symptoms obtains some outside personal advantage from his illness. The most obvious illustration is that of victims of motor vehicle accidents whose symptoms may be consciously or unconsciously manufactured with a view to inflating the damages or compensation to be claimed. Or, the symptoms may serve as an excuse for failure in a career, or even for not continuing in an occupation found to be burdensome and exacting.

[2] Nor do the categories embrace the following: (a) the 'inhibition' occurring where one type of a nerve cell in the brain tends by its synaptic action on other nerve cells to prevent the discharge of impulses; (b) in the case of educational processes, inhibitions in regard to learning and memory; or (c) the defensive inhibition in traumatic neuroses, e.g. involving paralysis.

Apart from primary and secondary gains, the process of symptom formation may reach a stage where, by long repetition, the symptom becomes so to speak fused with the ego, and indispensable to it. Some psycho-analysts take the view that the symptom has then become a goal, in its own right, of the ego. This is different from saying that there are external advantages from the continuance of the symptom.

In the case of obsessional practices, the continuance of the obsessional symptom may be nourished by the element of narcissistic gratification which the person concerned may feel. For example, a compulsive adherence to a set series of precautions may be regarded by him as proof of meticulousness and foresight. This has been said to apply also to obsessional rituals of cleanliness, which may be considered as proof of superior hygiene.

Finally, both modern psychiatry and psycho-analytic doctrine have destroyed the long prevalent myth that a symptom is a disease in itself, rather than an expression of some wider pathological condition of the person affected (see Appendix III). In the clinical area, psycho-analytic experience is indeed that even the elucidation of a particular symptom by making the patient aware of the unconscious reasons for that symptom does not invariably provide complete relief from it.[3] Such limited elucidation may fail to reach deep enough to other more serious conflicts in the unconscious, so that fresh symptoms may arise in the place of the symptom that has responded to treatment.

Symptomatic acts

The expression 'symptomatic act' was coined by Freud to describe certain acts or omissions upon the part of healthy persons as well as of neurotic persons, and which are usually more unobtrusive than symptoms in the strict sense, although they are similarly of the nature of a compromise-formation. The compromise, if it can be

[3] There is also the point that a particular symptom may be *overdetermined,* that is to say caused by a combination of several unconscious factors operating simultaneously, so that merely making the patient aware of one of such factors will not necessarily lead to the disappearance of the symptom. The concept of overdetermination of symptoms was one of the very earliest of Freud's contributions to psycho-analytic doctrine; see, e.g., his paper of 1896, 'The Aetiology of Hysteria', *Complete Psychological Works of S. Freud,* Vol. III, p. 216. The concept of overdetermination applies also to psychical errors and parapraxes; see, e.g., Freud's paper of 1898, 'The Psychical Mechanism of Forgetfulness', op. cit., Vol. III, p. 294.

termed such, is one between some suppressed sexual wish or attitude, on the one hand, and the claims of reality, on the other. The best-known symptomatic acts are those of losing or mislaying wedding or engagement rings, where there is a suppressed desire for intimacy with someone other than the husband or fiancé. Such a symptomatic act symbolizes really a hidden wish or fantasy.

Psycho-analytical theory with regard to dreams

Although like neurotic symptoms, dreams are compromise-formations, they are not necessarily pathological phenomena. One of Freud's most significant contributions to psycho-analytical doctrine was his formulation of principles governing the interpretation of dreams. His approach was consistently one of mental determinism, reflecting a firm belief that what appeared in dreams was traceable ultimately to some basic psychic material, to be found in the unconscious.

The impression may be gained from the psycho-analytical literature that the interpretation of a patient's dreams is a central part of analytical therapy. This is not entirely correct. Much depends on who the analyst is, and on the nature of the patient's specific disorder. It is understood that some analysts do not attach capital importance to dream interpretation as an element in the therapeutic process. This is partly because the patient's natural desire to receive an authoritative interpretation of the dream may oblige his analyst to given an explanation which he is reluctant to give—it may not be helpful. Sometimes, such a dream interpretation may ring hollowly and artificially, while it may have little bearing upon the understanding of the unconscious forces which have brought about the patient's condition. Some analysts indeed believe that the recital of dreams of the previous night may hamper free associations being given by the patient.

Yet some dreams which reflect the emotional relationship of the patient to the analyst may be of value for therapeutic purposes. It has been well said that a patient dreaming is in a similar psychic state to a patient lying on a couch. But the analogy cannot be carried too far, because the patient's free associations may be interrupted by the analyst's observations, while a patient's dreams continue without interruption.

Freud introduced three concepts: (a) the manifest dream-content, corresponding to the train of images constituting the dream; (b) the latent dream-thoughts, or psychic material found by interpretation to lie beneath the dream; and (c) the dream-work, or process which converts the latent dream-thoughts into the manifest dream-content. These concepts seem to be more of descriptive, than of practical value.

Dreams can mirror profoundly the characteristics of the unconscious. They are proof of the boundless memory of the unconscious, of its store of symbolism, and of the extent to which impressions of early childhood have left irremovable traces. Freud has also penetratingly pointed out that the archaic and primeval elements in the unconscious, having no connection with the memories, fantasies, or impressions there embedded, can also be expressed in the dream-content. This explains partly why, from time to time, water appears in a person's dream as a symbol of birth or re-birth.

So generally influential has Freud's theory of dream interpretation been that his basic proposition that the dream-content so often represents an actual or disguised wish-fulfilment is now virtually non-controversial. Those who have day-dreams or day-fantasies, not far removed from dreams at night, will not need to be convinced of the wish-fulfilment nature of the dream content.

But the dream-content is not limited to the fulfilment of castles-in-the-air wishes. Repressed wishes, from which the dreamer's ego would recoil, are also satisfied. For example, in dreams of the deaths of parents, repressed infantile death wishes against them find gratification. Such an interpretation of the dream may be found repugnant, but the unconscious cannot be belied. So also with repressed sexual wishes, when these are satisfied in dreams, there is in effect a partial discharge of the related sexual tension.

The dream-content is also characterized, or perhaps put more correctly, conditioned by another operative factor, namely repetition-compulsion. This means that there is a tendency in dreams to reproduce again and again the pattern of impressions and wishes forgotten and repressed, or some previous strong emotional experience. Hence, the dream-content may include material not of the nature of a wish-fulfilment. This is perhaps demonstrated by the so-called 'comfort dream', in which a person dreams that he may miss catching a particular railway train, or that he has not done sufficient studying for a particular set of examinations, or that there is some other possibility of failure. Analysis shows that the person concerned has had in the past some similar experience in which he surmounted the possibility of failure.[4] In obedience to the law of repetition-compulsion, the 'comfort dream' usually appears time

4 Hence the implication in the 'comfort dream' is that the dreamer will nevertheless avoid failure.

and again with the same imagery corresponding to the particular earlier experience. The continued reproduction also of highly charged impressions and experiences of childhood is further proof of the repetition-compulsion trend in the dream-content.

Some further comment on the concept of repetition-compulsion is appropriate. Repetition-compulsion is a general tendency of the psyche, conditioned by the instincts, and is not necessarily confined to the re-animation in dreams of earlier experiences. But insofar as it operates upon unconscious wishes, conflicts, and traumatic memories, the force underlying the compulsion to repeat is, in theory, primarily due to the fact that the wishes, conflicts, and memories were repressed, and thus shielded from the influence of the ego.[5] It is characteristic of repetition-compulsion that emotions of unpleasure or anxiety may be repeated, however unwelcome to the personality.

Some psycho-analysts are of the view that dreams are not only governed by wish-fulfilment or influenced by repressed wishes, but may also be conditioned by the memory of some traumatic experience of special significance, and which is not necessarily repressed. The 'comfort dream' provides some support for this view.[6]

Examination of the imagery, both visual and auditory, in dreams reveals disguises or distortions of reality, and what are known technically as condensations and displacements of ideas and attitudes. The disguises or distortions may be briefly dealt with. Real persons, such as the analyst himself, for example, are represented in dreams by some other figure of the same symbolic significance. Symbols also serve to disguise the unconscious repressed elements of sexuality and aggressivity.

By condensation, a number of ideas and attitudes are fused into one. Hence a woman's dream of falling from an altitude can represent a merger of at least two ideas, i.e. failure in achieving a particular ambition, and succumbing to seduction.

A displacement is a transference of an emotional attitude from one idea or person to another idea or person. For example, death wishes against a parent, experienced in infancy, but repressed, may be re-enacted in a dream in which the analyst has become the target, and it is dreamed that he is dead.

[5] See H. W. Loewald, 'Some Considerations on Repetition and Repetition-Compulsion', *International Journal of Psycho-Analysis*, Vol. 52 (1971), p. 58, at p. 61.

[6] Cf. Freud's *Complete Introductory Lectures on Psychoanalysis*, pp. 274-275.

It can be seen then that, according to psycho-analytical doctrine, dreams serve to confer some primary gain on the dreamer by way of gratification or relief, in the same way as neurotic symptoms. This is true even of anxiety dreams, which may partially relieve a dreamer of his unconscious sense of guilt, at least during the course of the dream.

Against this truly scientific, albeit pessimistic theory of a dream world serving limited purposes but reflecting the deepest and most hidden desires of the unconscious, little has been advanced in a period now of over seventy years to refute Freud's basic conclusions. In several respects, these conclusions have been confirmed and almost rendered unchallengeable. One cannot always agree with the psycho-analytical decodings of dreams, and indeed psycho-analysts themselves would probably disagree in their interpretations. Yet this is of minor importance when considered in relation to the validation of Freud's main propositions.

Chapter VII

THERAPEUTIC VALUE OF PSYCHO-ANALYSIS: THE NEUROSES AND THEIR TRACTABILITY

Contrary to common belief, psycho-analytical therapy operates within a narrow field. It is not, and ought not to be regarded as a kind of cure-all for every type of mental and neurotic disorder. To some extent it covers a field wider than psychiatry strictly speaking, but at the same time it does not trespass on many areas to which psychiatry is applicable.[1] Nor does it exclude other means of treatment. At first sight, this may seem contradictory. There is a great body of psycho-analytic doctrine which seems so comprehensive in the range of its explanations of the structure of personality, and of the dynamics of the unconscious mind. And yet the fact remains that the therapeutic techniques devised by psycho-analysis can cope successfully with only certain limited categories of neurotic illnesses, such as the neuroses, hysteria, and some of the milder non-psychotic emotional states.[2] Even then the recovery of the patient is dependent upon the existence of favourable conditions. With regard to other types of mental illnesses, psycho-analysis can make some contribution towards the elucidation of their origins, and may in some cases mitigate their acuteness, without ensuring recovery. The effort to make further progress in the clinical area is unceasing.

This may seem a pessimistic view, but it ought not to be taken

1 See H. Flournoy, *La Psychanalyse, Les Médecins et le Public,* Geneva 1924, pp. 32-4.

2 Leaving aside the conditions that may be remediable by the various techniques of child analysis.

as negating the soundness of the basic theories of psycho-analysis. Apart from this, it must be remembered that some non-analytical psychiatric techniques are to some extent oriented towards psycho-analysis in the sense that they are based in a certain measure upon analytical concepts and criteria. Then as the science of medicine amply demonstrates, our ability to explain the origins of, and elucidate the symptoms of a particular disease does not necessarily involve a capability of curing persons of it, but sometimes at best only to prevent deterioration and to enable individuals affected to lead a more or less normal life; a good example is diabetes.

An analysis usually calls for three to five sessions of one hour each, per week, extending over a minimum span of six months. Some analyses may extent into years of treatment. The basic technique is that of free association by the patient, coupled with observation or explanation by the analyst as the case may require. Free association, that is, saying or describing uninhibitedly everything which passes through one's mind, without omission—this is the so-called 'Fundamental Rule' of analysis—is the very foundation of therapy. For one thing, it is because the patient ceases to control his thoughts and fantasies that clues can be provided concerning the nature of the unconscious conflicts governing the symptoms of his illness. Taken over a period of time, what has happened is that the analyst has made a scientific clinical investigation of a vast body of mental data peculiar to the patient. If for no other reason, the value of this protracted testing lies in its thoroughness.

The length of time, however, serves certain purposes other than that of meticulousness, and one such purpose is to produce the transference (see Chapter VIII) in relation to the analyst, casting upon him the feelings and reactions towards other persons who played a significant role in the patient's childhood or past. One of the points frequently overlooked by the public is that the patient must throughout be served only by the one analyst. This is partly because of the importance of the transference situation, and as we shall see difficulties arise when a patient is half-way through the course of treatment, and the analyst dies.

Object of psycho-analytical therapy

It is not the object of psycho-analytical therapy to convert a neurotic into a completely adjusted individual having full control of his mind. The more modest aim is to enable him to become aware of the repressed tendencies or attitudes behind his illness and to be at terms with these, conditioning his behaviour accordingly. Psycho-analysts cannot undertake to re-structure personalities. The patient may emerge wiser, and more stable, but basic personality characteristics will as a rule be unaffected.

Nor is it the purpose of psycho-analytical therapy to correct the single symptom, and then let the patient go. For example, if a patient is suffering from a particular obsessional thought, the treatment would not be regarded as complete if, although the thought has disappeared, the patient still remains unconscious of repressed tendencies, which could lead to other symptoms being manufactured.

In order to become aware of unconscious repressed tendencies, it is not sufficient for the patient to be told that they exist. A 'working out' process is necessary. Through hours of free association, guided by observations and interpretations of the analyst, the patient becomes truly conscious of the unconscious attitudes at the root of his illness. Over and above this awareness, his ego requires strengthening, while he may need also to come to terms with the defence mechanisms in the ego. Therefore, although the patient cannot be given a new personality, he may find himself adopting sounder and more reasonable attitudes less likely to produce conflicts between his ego and unconscious tendencies.

Other conditions must be met if the treatment is to be successful. There must be the right kind of *rapport* between patient and analyst. It is bad, for instance, if a patient is overawed by his analyst, and unable freely to associate thoughts related to his childhood because this might reveal the fact that his social origins were inferior to those of the analyst. If the patient has to choose the analyst with care, it is no less true that the analyst must be satisfied with the patient. A patient must have sufficient intelligence to undergo analysis and to co-operate in the procedure. At some phases of the analysis, there must be unreserved co-operation, particularly where the patient is told by the analyst that he is equipped to face situations in which he was previously stricken with attacks of anxiety or suffered other emotions. Non-collaboration with the analyst in these crucial stages may rob subsequent analytical sessions of much of their value and meaning.

The surrounding circumstances must also, to some extent, be favourable. It is difficult to strengthen the ego at the same time as the patient is being discouraged by other matters, such as failure in his career, or matrimonial troubles, or continued physical ill-health.

For psycho-analysts, it is all important for the patient to come up with resistances in the course of the treatment. The resistances are the key to the understanding of the unconscious tendencies that have produced his illness. A smooth analysis, with no perceptible resistances would be highly suspect by psycho-analysts.[3]

The burden which generally falls upon an analyst should be viewed with sympathy. Strictly speaking, he is dealing only with the neurotic disorder of a single individual, but often his task may be, for practical purposes, to solve a grave family crisis centring round the neurosis of a parent or child. Nor can he produce immediate results. A long continued analysis may be necessary while the family crisis deepens and widens.

In this connection a major difficulty is the factor of expense. As a rule, analysts do not underrate the importance of this matter, although they are not inclined to admit that it may account for some therapeutic failures. Where a patient is not making progress, and is paying substantial amounts which he cannot really afford in fees, his sense of guilt may be accentuated. Further improvement may cease. It is said that if the patient is not obliged to pay, he will lose the incentive to treat his analysis seriously, but this usually is not true where the patient really has the will to recover. Many patients have been treated without charge, and it is not believed that the results were worse, taken as a whole, than in the case of patients who had to pay fees.

When all these limiting factors and conditions are borne in mind, it is right to say that too much should not be expected of an analysis, or of an analyst.

Length of the analysis

A protracted analysis creates problems other than that of expense. It may tend to defeat rather than to promote recovery. First, there is the aspect that the patient becomes psychically dependent on the analyst, and this dependence may be of such a degree as to enfeeble the ego. Second, the very length of the treatment may aggravate the patient's sense of guilt. Third, some patients cease to be able to give free associations, because of a lurking feeling that in years of sessions all the psychic material of any significance must have

[3] Five forms of resistance have been identified: (1) repression resistance; (2) transference resistance; (3) resistance flowing from the secondary gain involved in the illness; (4) resistance due to the unconscious need for punishment, the illness representing the punishment; and (5) repetition-compulsion resistance. See Robert Waelder in *The Psychoanalytic Quarterly*, Vol. XXXVI (1967), at p. 9.

been exhausted, and because they find themselves repeatedly going over the same ground.

The psychic dependence may become so rooted that the sessions are of significance to the patient only as a means of uplifting morale and diminishing anxiety, and no real analytic work is being done. In that event, the analysis itself has become the illness, and should preferably be terminated, so that the patient may not further enfeeble his ego. If terminated, this does not mean that all contact should henceforward be broken between the patient and the analyst, but simply that futile analytical sessions ought not to be continued. The patient may well find that he has had sufficient therapy to be able to stand on his own feet and that all he needs is to see the analyst once or twice during the year, with regard to special difficulties.

Advantages of psycho-analytical therapy

Successes and failures are part of the stock-in-trade of every psycho-analyst, but to be quite fair, it must be admitted that many cases of non-recovery are not absolute failures; that is to say, although complete cures were not effected, analysis was at least effective to ward off a grave psychic breakdown, or to alleviate suffering and to enable the patient to continue working at his occupation.

The failure of an analysis may be inexplicable in some cases. Nor is it easy to devise scientifically unobjectionable methods for investigating analytical failures and successes, with a view to drawing inferences regarding the reasons for non-recovery.[4] One difficulty at the outset is how to determine whether the analysis has really failed.

Also, it would be unjust to psycho-analysts to put the blame on them for all analytical failures, or to criticize them for continuing with treatment which would foreseeably not succeed. Often success was almost achieved, while in other cases the analyst acted correctly in persevering with therapy, in order to mitigate the illness, which in itself was a worth-while result.

As against the lack of success which is one of the risks, and as against the various limiting factors in the treatment, such as expense, length of time, and the patient's intelligence, there must be measured the concrete advantages of psycho-analytical therapy.

4 Cf. Michael Scriven, 'The Experimental Investigation of Psycho-analysis' in Sidney Hook (ed.), *Psychoanalysis* . . . , pp. 226-51.

A major initial benefit to a patient is the general 'cleansing' of his personality, through the process of free association, in respect to unpleasant and repugnant thoughts and memories. This cathartic effect ought to be considered as a gain. In addition to the aspect of relief given by the feeling that there is nothing abnormal or perverted in the various ideas and fantasies emerging in his free associations, the ego has also been permanently strengthened.

If the analysis has been successful, the patient's gain has been even greater. For inasmuch as according to psycho-analytical doctrine the repressed tendencies are the core of the illness, no therapy can conceivably be as effective as the analytical technique in dealing with these tendencies, for it makes the patient conscious of what was hidden from him, and enables him to come to terms with the subject-matter of his former repressions. The displacement of repressions is the central therapeutic aim from which the analyst does not deviate.

For this reason, the value of even partial successes in analysis is not to be minimized. A partial displacement of repressions, with a concomitant strengthening of the ego, represents a therapeutic gain. The partial stabilization has prevented a greater deterioration. It also represents a mitigation of suffering. A curious fact, too, is that sometimes the apparently unlucky patients, only partially cured, may make surprising further progress, following a period of difficulty experienced immediately after the termination of analytical sessions.

Many patients have been disappointed or disillusioned after psycho-analytical treatment because it did not provide the complete cure they hoped for, and dreamed of. This particularly applies to the ambitious ones, who looked to analysis to give them a mental edge over possible competitors, and a greater ability to withstand strains. They expected miracles. In all honesty, they would be obliged to admit that their condition had been alleviated. Yet their point of view has to be appreciated; they may have paid considerable fees for what seems a disproportionately negligible result. In rejoinder, one would have to ask what alternative therapies would have met their case. In a great number of instances the answer would be that analytical treatment was the only therapy which could alleviate their symptoms.

It remains an unfortunate fact that the treatment of neurotic disorders, whether by psycho-analysis or non-analytical psychiatry, is an expensive process.

With regard to comparisons unfavourable to psycho-analysis upon a rate-of-recovery basis for (a) analytically treated patients and (b) untreated persons making spontaneous recoveries, it is felt that such comparisons do not sufficiently take into account the fact that the analytically treated patients must have had some desire for this form of therapy. They may at least have felt a pressing necessity for treatment. On the balance of probabilities, then, they might have become worse without treatment. There is some evidence, also, to show that the spontaneous improvements in untreated persons suffering from neurotic disorders do not for the most part represent results comparable with those corresponding to the inner permanent gain, however partial, achieved through psycho-analytic therapy.

The neuroses and their tractability

We may turn now to consider the question of the tractability of neuroses, which represent such a major proportion of the mental disorders treated by psycho-analysts.

As in the case of the word 'inhibition', the expressions 'neurosis' and 'neurotic' have come to receive a wider meaning, according to behavioural and other philosophers, than according to psycho-analytical doctrine. They have been taken to include emotional dissatisfactions, vague worries and conditions of malaise, and the currently common symptom of a feeling of inability to find any sense in life. Persons suffering from these states have also sought psycho-analytical therapy, but this does not mean that a psycho-analyst would characterize their complaints as neuroses. It is important, both theoretically and clinically, to maintain a clear distinction between the neuroses and such other conditions.

The precise nature and meaning of the specifics in a neurosis continue to be elusive, even for psycho-analysts. The main hypotheses formulated by Freud may be assembled as follows: (a) the neuroses are inhibitions in the development of the libido; (b) infantile fixations are in many cases decisive of the form of a neurosis; (c) neurotic symptoms are the outcome of a conflict between the repressed wishes or tendencies and the forces opposing gratification; (d) quantitative considerations determine whether the conflict terminates in a neurotic disorder or is resolved in a healthy manner; (e) the conditions for a neurosis exist when infantile anxiety, as a reaction to unconscious wishes or tendencies, continues to hold its station in the personality;[5] and (f) contributing factors in the development of neuroses are the lengthy stage of infantile helplessness and need of parental love, coupled with the two phases of sexuality, infantile and post-latency. The tendencies, subject of the conflict, can also include repressed aggressive urges.

This generalized picture of a neurosis tells us nothing, however, of some of the points which are so important for the success of psycho-analytical therapy; among such crucial factors are the intensity of the infantile fixations, the strength of the repressing forces, the inherited constitutional make-up of the neurotic patient, the degree of intelligence that he possesses, and his developed attitudes and character traits which have had some fringe influence on the manner in which he has hitherto coped with repressed impulses. In addition, there is the severity of the neurosis as a whole to be considered, for it may have developed into a serious flight from reality.

An impression may be gained from the psycho-analytical literature, particularly the early literature on the subject, that all neuroses are in principle amenable to psycho-analytical therapy. This is a widespread view and accounts for the fact that many persons, afflicted with neurotic symptoms, approach psycho-analysts in all confidence that they will be cured.

The fact is that neuroses are relatively intractable when treated by psycho-analysis, and the word 'intractable' here means not merely incurable, but remediable, if at all, by dint of protracted time-consuming effort. The therapeutic difficulties spring from the special characteristics of a neurosis, as described above. In order to treat the neurotic patient, these characteristics must be dealt with. There must be an undoing of fixations, a dislodging of repressions, and a replacement of infantile anxieties by a mature appreciation of the wishes and tendencies in the unconscious. As mentioned in an earlier chapter, the obstacle of an unconscious sense of guilt may also be present, coupled with an unfulfilled need for punishment, which finds gratification in the illness. Another ever present difficulty in neuroses is the strength of identifications with parents or parent-figures, which make it difficult for the analyst to influence the course of treatment. The remarks made by Freud in this connection are appropriate:

[5] Note Robert Waelder's paraphrase of Freud's views: 'The essence of the neurotic . . . appears to be the retention or reanimation of past and obsolete conditions of anxiety'. See *The Psychoanalytic Quarterly,* Vol. XXXVI (1967), p. 7.

> In quite a number of the various forms of nervous illness, in the hysterias, anxiety-conditions, obsessional neuroses, our hypothesis proves sound. By seeking out the repression in this way, discovering the resistances, indicating the repressed, it is actually possible to accomplish the task, to overcome the resistances, to break down the repression, and to change something unconscious into something conscious. As we do this we get a vivid impression of how, as each individual resistance is being mastered, a violent battle goes on in the soul of the patient.[6]

What happens, however, if the neurosis is a stubborn condition, and the patient is, notwithstanding psycho-analytical treatment, still left with a residue of neurotic symptoms? This practical question seldom receives emphasis in the literature of psycho-analysis. But the answer is that, having reached the end of the line, the patient must learn to accept and to live with his partial neurosis, much as in the same way a diabetic is obliged to adapt himself to a permanent physiological impairment. It is a compromise with reality, but one which can usually be borne, provided that the patient continues to work consistently at some occupation. After a certain time, it will dawn on him that the analytical sessions have not been entirely devoid of therapeutic value.

[6] See Freud's *General Introduction to Psychoanalysis,* p. 380.

Chapter VIII

TRANSFERENCE AND COUNTER-TRANSFERENCE

The transference situation which occurs in the course of a psychoanalytical treatment is regarded as being essential for the termination of the treatment, and for the patient's recovery. It may be defined as the emotional relationship which develops on the part of the patient towards the analyst after some progress has been made beyond the early phases of the analysis. There are two mental processes or mechanisms involved in the development of a transference. One such process is that of displacement, and as we have seen in an earlier chapter, this consists in the transfer of an emotional attitude from a particular person or idea to another, generally speaking, similar person or similar idea. Theoretically, the patient is considered to project his infantile emotions and attitudes towards his parents on the analyst as a substitute for the parents. The other mechanism which brings about a transference situation is that of repetition-compulsion—that tendency to repeat earlier emotional attitudes and experiences, provided that they were significant. In this instance, the law of repetition-compulsion unconsciously constrains the patient to repeat the emotional pattern of infancy, without such repetition involving conscious recollection on his part. This point of non-recollection is important, because it means that a responsibility is cast upon the analyst to interpret the transference relationship to the patient in such a way that he gains conscious insight regarding the wishes and tendencies of early childhood as they appear in the guise of the transference situation.

The law of repetition-compulsion applies to the impulses and urges of the id, as well as to the defensive mechanisms and measures within the ego against the forces of the id. Hence, the transference situation consists of an amalgam of the reproduction of two categories of infantile psychological experiences. The first are emotional impulses and attitudes stemming from the id and directed against parents or parent-figures. These infantile emotions include fear, love, hate, jealousy, and contempt, coupled with the anxiety centred around, or fused with these feelings. Second are the defence mechanisms and defences cast up by the ego in the patient's infancy as against instinctual urges, whether erotic or aggressive. Thus, it is suggested that patients will reproduce a submissive, feminine, love-demanding attitude developed towards the father by way of defence against infantile aggressive feelings experienced in respect to him.

In the transference situation, there may be repeated not only feelings or attitudes experienced during infancy *towards* parents or parent-figures, but also concomitant emotions and reactions which are not directed against any persons, but are felt inwardly. An illustration is the sense of guilt which, originally compounded of a fear of punishment and tension associated with the thought that a parent's love may be lost, comes to be subsequently internalized.

Transference situation represents a new neurosis

The transference situation, according to psycho-analytical theory, represents a new, artificially developed neurosis, not based upon the actual position of the patient in relation to his analyst, but a re-enactment in a different milieu of the former infantile neurosis, which lies at the seat of the patient's neurotic disorder. While it is a repetition of the earlier emotional composite, it is at the same time of the nature of a regression by the patient to infantile attitudes.[1] The phenomenon of regression to the emotional position of infancy can arise in other ways. For example, a person may become a member of a closely integrated community of individuals, subject to a leader who comes to represent the re-externalized super-ego, so that the person concerned regresses to the phase antedating the formation of conscience.

It cannot be said that the analyst deliberately engineers the transference situation, but the situation is nevertheless somewhat of an artificial creation. On the one hand, there is the situation of dependence, where the patient with trust and confidence in the

[1] Naturally in the case of child analysis, such a kind of transference neurosis cannot arise in the course of analysis of young children. The analytical technique here will depend very much more on the analyst's direct relationship with the child under analysis.

analyst, submits himself to treatment by the one man or woman over a lengthy period, during which he must rely absolutely upon his physician. Then, there are duties of correct behaviour imposed upon him during the course of the analysis: punctual and regular attendance at the hour-long analytical sessions, obedience to the fundamental rule of free association requiring him not to withhold from expression any thoughts which may be repugnant or repulsive, and payment of fees. In addition, he is required to co-operate with the analyst at various phases of the progress of the treatment, when he may be called upon to face situations of anxiety or otherwise, from which he had previously recoiled.

Is the transference relationship a consciously felt situation, so far as the patient is concerned? It is difficult to give an answer which will meet all cases. Undoubtedly, the basis of the situation is unconscious, being composed of those elements or processes of displacement, repetition-compulsion, and regression already referred to. A patient will then work up strong feelings towards the analyst, which rest upon that unconscious basis, but those feelings will of course be consciously experienced. Often they are disguised or distorted into likes or dislikes of the analyst for reasons related to his present situation, and not apparently reflecting the ambivalent feelings of infancy towards parents. The very intelligent patient, who has previously read books on psycho-analysis, and who is well-informed about the transference situation, represents a special case. There will be a tendency in such a patient to fight against a regression to an infantile emotional relationship, and if, none the less, the unconscious force of repetition-compulsion prevails, the patient will be conscious to some extent of what is happening in his attitude towards the analyst.

Interpretation of the transference situation

The transference situation is a tool to be used by the psycho-analyst for enabling the patient to overcome his resistances, and to undo repressions. The psycho-analyst's role is primarily one of interpretation—to demonstrate to the patient that in his emotional involvement with the physician, he is reliving an earlier infantile situation in a disguised form. In theory, if the patient can be made aware of this, then this opens the way to conscious insight of the fact that repressions developed in infancy have contributed to his neurotic condition. It is also said that the transference situation provides a source of information for the analyst himself, but this must depend of course upon the diagnostic skill and length of experience of the analyst. If the analyst is sufficiently competent and experienced, he generally has an accurate conception of the origins of the patient's neurosis after a few weeks of analytical sessions, without having to rely upon what is thrown up in the course of the transference.

All this however conveys the impression that interpretation of the transference situation follows a smooth course, with the patient gradually becoming convinced of the truth of the understanding which the analyst has induced in him. This is not necessarily so. A highly charged transference can involve a strong resistance on the part of the patient, with often deep resentment against the analyst threatening the successful outcome of the treatment. In certain instances, this climax is not surmounted. The patient may temporarily become worse, and treatment may be broken off. A very experienced analyst can frequently foresee with certain patients that the transference will be a complication, rather than an aid, and will not be willing to treat them for this reason.

On the other hand, where these difficulties do not arise, the transference situation really represents the core around which recovery takes place. The advantages then outweigh all disadvantages. The repressions can be displaced, and the treatment achieves its goal.

Moreover, even if the treatment falls down over the transference, this does not mean that the transference is devoid of value. In some cases, the patient who has left the treatment will in course of time gain insight into what occurred, and will be benefited.

Is the transference indispensable?

A natural question to ask is whether the transference situation is really essential for therapeutic success. The psycho-analytical literature is now heavily weighted in favour of the more usual necessity of the transference in therapeutic technique. It is said also that therapy cannot be of much avail where the patient is incapable of producing a transference to mirror his significant infantile attitudes and wishes.

However, there are two practical situations which can arise. Both involve difficulty if it is to be assumed that usually the transference is indispensable for recovery. Firstly, the analyst may die while the patient is in mid-stream in the course of the transference situation and before he has gained proper conscious insight into the significance of the transference. Secondly, owing to war or other contingencies, the patient may have to break off treatment with a particular analyst and go to another country. This may occur before the transference situation has been properly unfolded and resolved.

Under these circumstances, the alternatives for the patient are either not to resume analytical treatment with another analyst, and be content with results already achieved, or to seek out another analyst. If he does not recommence analytical treatment, it is always possible that, as mentioned above, he will in progress of time acquire a degree of insight in respect to the meaning of the transference situation, as he has experienced it, however incompletely.

If he does resume analytical treatment, it must be left to the new analyst to decide in what manner therapy is to proceed, and naturally regard will be paid to the progress achieved with the first analyst. If transference were so indispensable as claimed, the situation would be somewhat unsatisfactory from the patient's standpoint, for in effect he has lost the benefit of insight into a transference brought only after many hours of analytical work. However, it is believed that in some cases at least, this has not proved to be a serious difficulty in the treatment by the new analyst.

Counter-transference

The question of the so-called 'counter-transference' of the analyst is closely related to the problem of the correct attitude to be exhibited by the analyst towards the patient.

It is maintained that the analyst should adopt an attitude of uncommitted neutrality—neither aloof nor disinterested. But by the same token he should not cease to be patient and tolerant, and concerned about the patient's welfare. By maintaining a balanced objectivity, he provides the right setting for a patient to come to terms with the tendencies and wishes at the root of his illness. This is important also for ensuring that the patient adheres to the fundamental rule of free association, and that the flow of material from free association continues. Some analysts believe that the patient should receive no assurances from the physician to relieve anxieties, allay a sense of guilt, or otherwise encourage him, because this might interfere with the 'working through' process of the analytical sessions. This rule is impossible to apply in the case of the severe anxiety states, as analysts with telephones should know. In any event, it is unacceptable as a generalization for all patients, because such a negative rule strictly applied would aggravate the sense of guilt of some patients. The requisite attitude of neutrality certainly obliges analysts not by words or attitude to aggravate a patient's sense of guilt.

The considerations which dictate that the analyst should be neutral make it imperative, correlatively, to avoid counter-transference. There are many directions in which a counter-transference may manifest itself. Curiously enough, it may often take the form of a projection on the patient of an attitude adopted by the analyst towards his own children, leading the analyst to adopt an unconsciously authoritarian attitude, which may cause the patient to be uneasy and hesitant about the self-revelatory disclosures to be made in the course of his free associations. Another illustration is that of unconscious exhibitionism, as for example where the analyst endeavours to show that he has superior linguistic ability, or a superior sense of humour, and so on. All such expressions of the counter-transference tend to produce disturbing emotional currents in the patient, possibly accentuating his sense of guilt, impairing free associations and the continued flow of material in the analytical sessions, and in some instances cutting across the development of the patient's own transference relationship towards the analyst.

Mere friendliness does not amount to counter-transference, for this is not and cannot be considered as an emotional reaction to the patient, but as a normally necessary attitude in the analyst-patient relationship. It has been suggested that one way for an analyst to alert himself to the possibility of counter-transference on his part is by self-analysis from time to time.[2]

The non-transference relationship

The relationship between patient and analyst cannot be wholly one of transference. At the outset of the analysis no transference has developed, and when in the course of time the process of re-animation and reconstitution of early infantile attitudes is in motion there will still be elements of the relationship between patient and analyst, which are not governed by early infantile feelings, and which are referable to current circumstances. This non-transference relationship, sometimes referred to as the 'real relationship', ought theoretically not to be present if there were rigidly perfect obser-

[2] O. Kernberg, in an interesting article 'The Concept of Countertransference', *Journal of the American Psychoanalytic Association,* Vol. 13 (1965), pp. 38-56, distinguishes two kinds of counter-transference: (a) the traditional counter-transference by way of reaction to the patient's transference; and (b) the 'totalistic' counter-transference, being a response to the totality of the patient's attitudes.

vance of the rule of impersonal attitude upon the part of the analyst, that is, the strict preservation of the so-called 'analytic incognito'.

The question is whether such a limited non-transference relationship is necessarily an obstacle to therapy. It has been claimed[3] that far from representing a bar to recovery, the evolution of a real relationship can be of therapeutic value, in addition to the interpretation of the transference. One of the grounds for this view is the fact that patients may feel the need for a real relationship, and be uneasy in an atmosphere where the analyst seeks to clothe himself with an aura of total anonymity. In any event, even if such total anonymity were desirable, it is more often than not unattainable in practice.

[3] See study by Ralph R. Greenson and Milton Wexler, 'The Non-Transference Relationship in the Psychoanalytical Situation', *International Journal of Psychoanalysis,* Vol. 50 (1969), pp. 27-38.

Chapter IX

SADISM, MASOCHISM, AND THE DEATH INSTINCT

As we have seen, Freud propounded the controversial hypothesis of a death instinct,[1] and according to the theories developed by him, there is a close interrelation between sadism and masochism and the death instinct. For this reason they are discussed together within one frame of reference in the present chapter. Although Freud's views have been, and are still, under attack, they are cogent and serve to explain much that seems otherwise obscure.

It is important to observe that Freud did not purport to enunciate a series of absolutes concerning sadism and masochism, or concerning the relationship of sadism and masochism to the death instinct. He was rather seeking to postulate, as a basis for further scientific investigation or as a philosophic assumption, a generalized theory of the instincts which covered not only the erotic urge, but the aggressive and destructive tendencies in man.

Definitions

A first step is to define broadly each of the three concepts or tendencies.

Sadism: Sadism represents a tendency of an aggressive character, directed outwards against others, for the purpose of inflicting pain, or involving an enjoyment of the fact that pain has been inflicted. In both instances, there is some gratification of sensuality from the fact that pain has been suffered by others. It will be noticed that the person with the sadistic tendency need not himself have inflicted

[1] See Chapters I and III and Freud's *An Outline of Psycho-Analysis*, pp. 5-9.

the pain, provided that the sensual desire that some other person has suffered pain is satisfied. Sadism may be conscious or unconscious.

Masochism: Masochism represents a tendency of an aggressive character, directed inwards against the self, so that the self experiences either physical or mental pain. As in the case of sadism, there is gratification of sensuality from the fact of suffering. The person with the masochistic tendency need not be his own torturer, provided that he has procured someone else to inflict the pain, or has otherwise brought about the situation from which pain is suffered, so that the pain can be said to be self-inflicted. As in the case of sadism, masochism may be conscious or unconscious.

Before defining the concept of the death instinct, there are two points to be made regarding these definitions of sadism and masochism.

The word 'pain' must be understood in a wide sense, as covering all kinds of suffering, including anxiety, disappointment, shame and humiliation, and other feelings of distress. And, although in both cases, the tendencies are said to be aggressive, the primary aspect may be the pleasure obtained from the infliction or receiving of pain.

Death instinct: The concept of the death instinct is that of an unconscious destructive tendency in every living human being, operating ultimately to restore that being to the primal state of inert matter. It is contrasted with the so-called 'life instinct' which, as Freud has well expressed, can 'vouch for the struggle to live on'.[2]

It has been said that Freud propounded the concept as a biological, and not as a psychic concept. This is not entirely correct, for he made reference to the 'introversion' of the death instinct, and to that extent, he appears to have been thinking in terms of the psychic consequences. Moreover, as we have seen in Chapter III, in his last formulation on the subject he divided the basic instincts into two—Eros and the death (or destructive) instinct—and referred to these as representing 'the somatic demands upon mental life'.[3]

General nature of sadism and masochism

Under psycho-analytic doctrine, sadism and masochism are generally presented as component tendencies of sexuality, with

[2] See Exchange of Open Letters, Albert Einstein-Sigmund Freud, p. 45.
[3] See *An Outline of Psycho-Analysis*, p. 5.

which there have come to be blended elements of aggressivity, directed outwards in the former case, and inwards in the latter.

Some writers on psycho-analysis have sought to maintain the proposition that, unlike other components of sexuality, neither tendency is connected with the parts of the body, including the erotogenic zones. This can scarcely be accepted as a generalization which is correct for all cases of sadism and masochism. Charges of assault, involving evidence of sadistic cruelty, in which the genitals have been beaten, have come before the courts from time to time. The sadistic flagellation of buttocks—as also the masochistic equivalent in the case of men—is a well-known practice. In regard to both sadism and masochism, anal eroticism plays a considerable role, as reflected in the evidence which frequently emerges in divorce cases. The Marquis de Sade regarded the anal eroticism of the sensually masochistic woman as a commonplace of the bedroom in eighteenth century France. The practice receives commendation in some of the sex manuals now currently available.

The central characteristic of both sadism and masochism is the blending of pain and pleasure. It has puzzled many why there should be such an amalgam. Freud, of course, had always made it clear that the sexual and aggressive instincts could work against each other, or blend.[4] Nor is the association of pain and pleasure altogether surprising. As illustrated in the example of anal eroticism, both the active and passive parties experience sensual feelings in the respective acts of inflicting and suffering pain. The blending of pain and pleasure also occurs in differing measures in normal sexual coitus. Besides, as has been seen in Chapter V, anxiety itself may become 'sexualized', so that repeated anxiety attacks are but expressions of sensuality.

One might think that, because sadism involves an active role, and masochism one which is passive, sadistic tendencies are the exclusive prerogative of the masculine sex, and masochistic tendencies appertain solely to the opposite sex. This is not so according to psycho-analytical doctrine. Women are capable of unconscious sadism, as is demonstrated frequently when feminine gossip becomes loaded with malice, and some women exhibit pleasure in hearing of the misfortunes or disappointments of other persons. Moreover, masochism is frequently not present in women except to a very slight extent, and even where women have unconscious masochistic tendencies, these may be accompanied by a repressed

[4] This was also true of Eros and the destructive (or death) instinct. See his *An Outline of Psycho-Analysis*, p. 6.

fear of masochism. Curiously enough, also, strongly developed masochistic tendencies are quite commonly found in men, and it is known that boys frequently have a feminine-masochistic attitude in relation to their fathers. This confirms Freud's point of the bisexual tendencies of boys.

There appear to be two views of the relationship between sadism and masochism. According to one theory, masochism is a derivative of sadism in the sense that it results from the person's self becoming the object against which sadistic tendencies are directed. Under a second theory, sadism springs from the seeds of masochism, because the masochist switches from his own self-inflicted pain to the notion of causing pain to others. He will gain pleasure from the masochistic identification of himself with the person on whom the pain has been inflicted. The truth seems to lie between the two. In some, masochism will result from an inward direction of sadistic tendencies, while in others sadism may be cultivated from an early beginning with masochistic identifications. What makes both situations possible is the plasticity of the sexual urges which can ally themselves, somewhat indiscriminately, either with an outward or inward directed aggressivity. This is sensuality enjoyed through the infliction of pain, as such, whether on the person concerned himself or on others, and such a tendency is perhaps rightly called a sado-masochistic tendency.

The analyst is confronted with a difficult task in trying to guide a sado-masochistic patient along the path towards awareness of his unconscious sadistic and masochistic impulses. The patient may dimly feel that there is a sensual basis for the infliction by him of pain on others, or for his own sufferings, but has a strong resistance to appreciating the full extent of this sensuality.

Relationship of sadism and masochism to the death instinct

For Freud, the destructive drive in the death instinct provided a key to the understanding of sadism and masochism. He regarded both tendencies as manifestations of the destructive drive, turned outwards in the case of sadism and inwards in that of masochism, allied in each case with an admixture of eroticism. In masochism, the introversion of the destructive drive is softened and mitigated by the presence of sensuality. Indeed Freud seems to have regarded the death instinct as a kind of catalyst for sensuality or pleasure. He put forward the view that where the destructive drive, not alloyed with sexuality as in the case of sadism, was directed outwards in its pure form, it was nevertheless accompanied with some degree of narcissistic enjoyment, because the wish of the ego for power was gratified. It was equally possible to say that where the ego was curtailed rather than confirmed in its power, as in the case of masochism, nevertheless the introversion of the destructive drive produced sensual satisfaction.

This, at first sight, provides a depressing, pessimistic picture of the central strivings of mankind, with no room for spirituality. Thus, the beauty of music and of the visual arts is brought within the scope of sensuality, being that erotic urge which vies with and may correct the death instinct. Yet the interplay of Eros and the death instinct contributes, according to Freud, to the development of human culture, so that to this extent there is a spiritual element in Eros. Freud agreed that his theory was 'a species of mythology and a gloomy one at that'[5]; however, he was prepared also to concede that there was room in this theoretical system for love, devoid of sexual intent, to provide some antidote to the destructive drive of the death instinct.[6]

Categories of sadism and masochism

It is possible to divide sadism and masochism each into two categories: actual and moral.

The categories of actual sadism, and of actual masochism can be subdivided into two classes: erotogenic and non-erotogenic. In erotogenic sadism and masochism, the sensual satisfaction is attached to the infliction on, or the receipt of pain by particular areas of the human body, which have some erotic significance; e.g. flagellation of buttocks. Non-erotogenic sadism and masochism consist of the infliction or receipt of pain, or humiliating or being humiliated, or causing distress or being subjected to distress, and so on, without sensuality attaching itself to parts of the human body. Nevertheless, the sensual element is still there. Examples are the sadistic judge who 'takes it out' of a young barrister committing a mistake through inexperience, and the masochist who tortures himself by fasting or other form of self-deprivation.

In moral sadism and moral masochism, the situation is somewhat different. The moral sadist, with a severe super-ego, by force of which unconscious sexual and other wishes have been repressed,

[5] See Exchange of Open Letters, Albert Einstein-Sigmund Freud, p. 46. On the pessimistic character of the death instinct theory, see A. Garman, 'Within the Realm of the Death Instinct', *International Journal of Psycho-Analysis,* Vol. 52 (1971), p. 145, at p. 153.

[6] Ibid., pp. 48-9.

directs the sadistic tendencies against a person who has been able to gratify the wishes which his own censorious super-ego will not permit. In a sense, the repressed wishes are satisfied through the pain inflicted on the object of the sadistic tendencies. It may well be said that the result is a sexualization of morality for the particular sadistic person concerned, or alternatively that there has been a partial release of the inhibiting forces in the super-ego. Moral masochism is a condition in which there is a conflict between the censorious super-ego and the repressed or conscious wishes, and as a result of the conflict the unconscious impulses, which require gratification in pain and suffering, ally themselves with the super-ego and come to be sadistically directed against the self. Here again there is a kind of sexualization of the morality of the super-ego, but it is the ego which is the object of infliction of pain, and which suffers in a sensual manner.

The death instinct, and the derivative destructive drive

Freud's hypothesis of a death instinct has been the subject of almost as much controversy and derision as his theories earlier received, because of the attention he gave sexuality in the development of personality. Certainly, the idea of an instinct aiming at death is startling. At the same time it seems to minimize the significance of reason and will in the human personality.

The death instinct involves the concept of an innate self-destroying force in living organisms, and as Freud pointed out, this could be thought of as operating silently within the particular organism concerned, or more feasibly as being diverted towards the external world, and manifesting itself in aggressiveness and destructiveness. It is this basic notion of a destructive drive, as a derivative of the death instinct, coupled with the dire effects of destructiveness so long as it continues to be internalized, that has had a profound effect for over three decades now on the development of psycho-analytical doctrine.

Under Freuds' conception, the death instinct, with its derivative in the destructive drive, is innate and inherent. Yet this inner compulsion to return to an earlier state of inanimate matter[7] has largely been conditioned, according to Freud, by the pressure of

[7] It is claimed that this inner tendency to return to the primitive earlier condition is an illustration of the concept of repetition-compulsion referred to in Chapters VI and VIII. In the contrary sense, it can also be put that the concept of repetition-compulsion supports the theory of a death instinct.

age-old mixed geological-biological factors. This is somewhat different from saying, as some scholars of adaptational human biology have done, that a destructive urge in the human species has arisen by way of response to an unfavourable environment where men had to act aggressively in order to survive. Freud was thinking of events far back in geological history, and not of a kindling of the destructive drive through adventitious circumstances in the environment.

Freud's hypothesis of the death instinct is depressing and pessimistic at first sight. But is it any more depreciatory of the role of the human species than certain other theories of a biological nature, such as the doctrine favoured by many that the governing purpose of human beings is procreation, and that all else is subordinate to this reproductive function? The death instinct hypothesis is no more negative than this theory.

As Freud implies, the externalization of the destructive drive is essential to prevent inner ruin, and to this extent the life instinct may operate to bring into play the tendency of self-preservation. It follows that any restriction upon the outward thrust of the destructive drive would mean an increase in the forces of inner destructiveness, with adverse results.

Are there any other ways, apart from this externalization, of mitigating the force of the destructive drive? One particular solvent of destructiveness, suggested by Freud, was love—neutralization through the libido. This view was put by him in an exchange of letters in 1932 with Albert Einstein, in the course of which he made a suggestion for an 'indirect method' of eliminating war and maintaining peace.[8] As he said:

> If the propensity for war be due to the destructive instinct, we have always its counter-agent, Eros, to our hand. All that produces *ties of sentiment* between man and man must serve us as war's antidote.

Freud suggested two ties of sentiment for this purpose: that men should act upon the adage, 'love thy neighbour as thyself'; and that there should be a widening of the identification between men, leading to a feeling of community. With regard to the second, he pointed out that the whole edifice of human society was founded in large measure upon identification. In addition to Freud's idea that love would be a solvent for the destructive drive, other psychoanalysts have proposed measures for 'de-aggressivization'.[9]

[8] Exchange of Open Letters, pp. 48-9.

[9] It was expressly said by Freud that outward action would rob the destructive drive of its inward aggressive force. See *An Outline of Psycho-Analysis,* p. 7.

It is controversial whether the theory of the death instinct plays any practical part in analytical therapy. Whether Freud himself intended that the theory should have any practical bearing upon the course of an analytical treatment is also open to question, although in his study, *Analysis Terminable and Interminable* (1937), he expressed the view that a negative reaction by a patient to therapy, together with certain other mental phenomena, might amount to indications traceable to the existence of the death instinct. In his last study of any length, *An Outline of Psycho-Analysis* (1939),[10] he also proclaimed, with reference to the death instinct, that 'the holding-back of aggressiveness is in general unhealthy and leads to illness'. Perhaps it is true that if the death instinct theory were discarded, psycho-analytical theory and therapy would not be fundamentally affected, but by some analysts the theory is regarded as of clinical value.[11]

In *Analysis Terminable and Interminable* (1937), Freud wrote:

> Only by the concurrent or mutually opposing action of the two primal instincts—Eros and the death instinct—never by one or the other alone, can we explain the rich multiplicity of the phenomena of life.

It is this balanced interplay indeed that is contributing to the cultural development of mankind, and which Freud himself regarded as one of the safeguards of peace.

By way of concluding, the following points may be made.

So far as Freud emphasized the adverse effects either of continued internalization or of ill-directed externalization of the destructive drive appertaining to the death instinct, his views have been confirmed by clinical data and by the events of over three decades since his death in 1939.

If, as has been claimed, Freud was unduly pessimistic about the destructive drive, and overlooked the possibilities of its neutralization, since explored by pyscho-analysts, nevertheless he must be given credit for the fact that he did stress the value of non-sexual love as a solvent of certain ills of mankind. It may appear ironic that he, derided for being the apostle of unalloyed sexuality, should have pleaded so earnestly for the cause of non-sexual love.

Freud's clarification of the nature of sadism and masochism, including in particular his emphasis on the aspect of gratification in both instances, still stands as a classic exposition of the characteristic mechanisms of the two tendencies.

10 Ibid., p. 7.

11 Cf. W. H. Gillespie, 'Aggression and Instinct Theory', *International Journal of Psycho-Analysis,* Vol. 52 (1971), p. 155, at p. 159.

Chapter X

THEORY OF SUBLIMATION; WORK AND ARTISTIC CREATIVITY

In its psycho-analytical meaning, sublimation[1] denotes the channelling of the sexual and aggressive drives in directions other than the primal aims of sexuality and aggressivity, and enabling those drives to find gratification *to some extent* in fulfilling certain non-instinctual aims.

A convenient starting point is to take Freud's published views on the subject which are predominantly related to sublimation of the libidinal urges. There are passages however in which he made reference to sublimation of the instincts as a whole, while in certain other passages it appears to be implied that aggressive impulses may be directed into appropriate external non-destructive channels. It is possible that the term 'sublimation' was deemed inappropriate for re-directing of aggressivity, while it was his view also that aggressive impulses were less adaptable and pliable than the erotic urges. Possibly, 'neutralization' is a more appropriate term for the de-channelling of aggressivity. The psycho-analytic literature shows, however, that the term 'sublimation' is still being used with regard to the aggressive drive.[2]

Dealing with Freud's theory regarding the sublimation of sexuality, his conception was that of deflection to aims of a 'social' character, which were deemed to be 'above' purely sexual

1 In the non-analytical sense, sublimation denotes a chemical process of purification by conversion into a gaseous state, and re-solidification. Figuratively, it came also to mean the action of purifying or refining.

2 See, e.g., J. Lampl-de Groot, 'Reflections on the Development of Psycho-analysis: Technical Implications in Analytic Treatment', *International Journal of Psycho-Analysis,* Vol. 50 (1969), p. 567.

aims.[3] The deflection was to involve a sequence of two steps, beginning with the abandonment of a sexual aim, followed by the adoption of a new, desexualized, socially more acceptable aim. Perhaps the word 'diversion' and 're-direction' are more apt respectively than the words 'abandonment' and 'adoption'. Moreover, sublimation was not to be accompanied by repression. Rather, repression was avoided, and the libidinal urge was unfolded in a new manner.

Numerous illustrations can be given of the sublimation of component libidinal urges into socially acceptable, de-sexualized activities; for example, the component of exhibitionism can be directed into a stage career, sexual curiosity into physiological research regarding the biology of sex, urethral eroticism into an interest in hydraulic engineering, and visual sensuality into the study of paintings and beautiful works of art.

Some authors have maintained that sublimation works in a smooth, frictionless manner, and this is a point which must be dealt with at the outset, for the notion is apparently conveyed that by this easy alternative all human beings may attain a higher, purer level, freed of the claims of sexuality.

We have first to explain how and why sublimation works. The answer is not easy. One theory is based upon the plasticity of the sexual urges. As Freud has pointed out, a sexual drive may easily become reversible, both as to the nature of the emotion and from subject to object; e.g. love can change into hate, and sadism may come to be turned against the self, thereby being converted into masochism. Moreover, the intensity of the urges is capable of infinite variations, and may be readily diminished or neutralized by factors such as illness, long hours of intellectual work, alcohol, and increased aggressivity. Another point of view is that many people can find a release of libidinal tensions in partial satisfaction of components of the sexual drive. Thus the component of curiosity regarding the human body may to some extent be satisfied by an interest or research in human physiology. Hence, as Freud pointed out, a certain proportion of libido will be discharged in sublimation.

In the measure that there is such a limited gratification of the libidinal urge, it is probably correct to say that repression is correspondingly avoided, with a reduction of the anxiety or tension, if any, due to repression.

Another question is that of the capacity to sublimate. It is a fact

[3] See Freud's *General Introduction to Psycho-Analysis,* p. 302.

that a great many people are unable to sublimate, and one of the key factors militating against the recovery of some neurotic patients is precisely this inability.

The impression that sublimation is, or can be an absolute substitute for sexuality, under all circumstances, is not correct, nor was it one intended to be conveyed by Freud, who was largely concerned with finding a psychic alternative to repression in order to mitigate neurotic suffering. Indeed, Freud's writings during the period preceding his death reflect considerable pessimism about cultures which enable a greater measure of sublimation at the cost of a more drastic denial of the direct satisfaction of instinctual aims.

Sublimation can be both conscious and unconscious. It is stated in the psycho-analytical literature that sublimation occurs unconsciously during the latency period, for the main reasons that the primal sexual urges are then dormant, and that the super-ego (including the ego-ideal) is then an established part of the personality, so that sublimation is both facilitated and required.

Relationship between sublimation and repression

Freud at one time advanced the proposition that repression taking place at an early period precluded the sublimation of the repressed impulse; but that after the removal of the repression, the way to sublimation was again free.

Probably, Freud was thinking in terms of a deeply repressed impulse, and his suggested law was intended to be of the nature of a tendency-statement, that is to say a generalization regarding a trend or disposition. For clearly, there are cases where the repression of impulses does not preclude sublimation of these. Much depends on the character of the person, the nature of the impulse which is repressed, the degree of repression, and the particular kind of sublimation which is in question. So, for instance, the fact that they have repressed homosexual impulses does not prevent many men from sublimating these to some extent by joining and participating in the activities of men's clubs. Freud's proposition applies with less force to repressed aggressive impulses, for generally speaking a person may sublimate these in active sport while still repressing them.

The inability to sublimate and the absence of any existing sublimation are frequently found in neurotic persons, suffering from repressions. To that extent Freud's proposition is valid. But it may be that the severity of the repression has produced this incapacity to sublimate, and the lack of sublimation.

It is probably true that sublimation alone will not undo repressions, and that this displacement cannot succeed without the 'working through' process of analytical treatment enabling the nature of the repressions to be brought to the consciousness of the patient. Sublimations can then complete the patient's cure.

Social acceptability of the sublimation activity

The criterion of social acceptability of the activity representing the sublimation raises some difficulty. Does social acceptability mean the approval of the great majority of the community, or only of a particular group? For example, exhibitionistic or narcissistic urges may be sublimated by joining groups, which adhere to particular cults, but these may not necessarily be approved by the community as a whole. Nor would it seem to matter whether the person concerned is following an isolated activity, in sublimation of some special component urge of the instincts. The decisive point is perhaps whether the activity is one not in conflict with the super-ego, so that any existing tension or neurotic condition is not aggravated.

Work

The subject of work is more frequently covered in the psycho-analytic literature, with reference to the theory of sublimation as affecting the choice of a particular career or occupation. Apart from the aspect of sublimation, work is an important consideration from the standpoint of therapy. Generally speaking there is an insistence upon the part of analysts that patients should continue to keep working. The significance of work when allied with analytic therapy is mainly threefold: cessation of work tends to increase the patient's sense of guilt; work operates to preserve a patient's narcissistic self-esteem; and the constancy of work prevents a weakening of the ego, allowing the unconscious to take over in aggravation of the patient's condition.

In this connection, it is worth mentioning that one of the most frequent conditions leading patients to analysis in the first instance is an inability to work, particularly to do intellectual work. Then also there are the patients whose symptoms consist of a lack of satisfaction in their work, and a sense of being unable to cope with it.

Leaving the question of sublimation in respect to specific occupations, the motive behind work is usually to gain a livelihood, and it is hardly possible to generalize about unconscious impulses in that connection, unless self-preservation be one such impulse.

Freud, perhaps rightly, abstained from any attempt to explore in detail the question of unconscious motives for work, and confined himself to the statement that work provided an opportunity for the discharge of various impulses, narcissistic, erotic, and aggressive. Certainly, of these, work does materially absorb aggressivity.

Artistic creativity

Artistic creativity is a special kind of work which has received some attention from psycho-analytical writers. There appears to be general agreement that artistic creativity represents a sublimation of libidinal energies, the object of the artist being to create something which is beautiful in subject-matter or form, and beauty itself being a concept with roots in sensuality.

Another approach is to relate the actual products of the artist's craftsmanship to his unconscious wishes. In his *Introductory Lectures on Psycho-Analysis* (delivered 1915-1917),[4] Freud dealt with one category of artist, with an introverted disposition little removed from neurosis, and with instinctual urges of a narcissistic and erotic nature, including a wish to be loved. He is without the power to gratify these urges in reality, and this leads to an attempt first to realise them in a life of fantasy, which might easily in other circumstances lead to neurosis through the clash with reality. However, this type of artist is generally blessed with a powerful capacity to sublimate libidinal energy, and instead of a life of fantasy leading to neurosis, this capacity finds concrete expression in his artistic creations. If he has sufficient ability to translate his visions and day dreams into pleasing works of art, the life of fantasy will ultimately become one of reality, because artistic success brings gratification of the narcissistic wish, and of the wish to be loved. In other words, for the artist, the creative process represents a method of wish-fulfilment.

It may also be said that for such an artist, creativity is his shield against neurosis. Continued artistic production is a solvent of neurotic disorder, including anxiety states. Indeed the motive to avoid anxiety is often the spur behind much artistic creation. By such creation, also, an artist may strengthen a sense of personal identity, which is subject to disturbance.

Not all artists are neurotic, or with dispositions little removed from neurosis. There are many who have come to terms with their

[4] Reproduced in *General Introduction to Psychoanalysis,* pp. 327-8.

unconscious wishes and fantasies, but are impelled to produce creative works in which these wishes and fantasies are expressed or reflected. Here, there is almost a conscious sublimation of exhibitionistic urges, with a desire to present to the world representations of the imagery of their unconscious.

Psycho-analytical insights can also be applied to the creations themselves, in order to explain the origin of some significant feature. As a general rule, the artist's work mirrors not only his conscious ideas, but the conflicts, wishes, fantasies, and memories reposing in his unconscious. In his classical study of Leonardo da Vinci, published in 1910, Freud was able to propound the view that the famous smile on Mona Lisa's face was a kind of reproduction of the memory retained by Leonardo of his mother's smile in earliest childhood. So one feature or component of an artistic work may represent in itself a highly emotional instance of creativity, conditioned by the deepest feelings of the artist.[5]

However, it is not correct that artistic creations can always be subjected to psycho-analytical interpretations with profitable results. Sometimes no such interpretations can be applied, or if they can, the interpretation must be one subject to qualifications and reservations, and taking account of circumstances unrelated to the emotional motivations of the artist. As Professor E. H. Gombrich has pointed out,[6] artistic and poetic creation frequently involves a

[5] Among other psycho-analytic interpretations of artistic creativity or of the artist, the following have been suggested: (a) that the artist's creations fulfil a cathartic function, similar to the relief from tension produced through free association; (b) that the imagery in his works includes unconscious symbols, to which emotional importance is attached, so that in some cases the pictorial representations may be assimilated to dreams; (c) that the artist seeks to compensate himself for inner frustrations and conflicts, including a lowered narcissistic self-esteem; (d) that by way of defence against the death instinct, his aim is to achieve immortality through his art; and (e) that the artist's constant need to create obeys the repetition-compulsion principle to the same extent as the symptoms neutralised by his artistic efforts. See in this connection Ernest Kris, *Psychoanalytic Exploration in Art,* London 1953; Anton Ehrenzweig, *The Psycho-Analysis of Artistic Vision and Hearing. An Introduction to a Theory of Unconscious Perception,* London 1953; symposium, *Entretiens sur l'Art et la Psychanalyse,* Paris and The Hague 1968; Michael D. Robbins, 'On the Psychology of Artistic Creativity', *Psychoanalytic Study of the Child,* Vol. XXIV (1969), pp. 227-51.

[6] See his article, 'Freud's Aesthetics', *Encounter,* January 1966, pp. 37-8, and also Ernest Kris, *Psychoanalytic Exploration in Art,* London 1953, pp. 20-21, on the limitations of the psycho-analytic explanation of art, including the explanation of artistic genius.

non-emotional, objective element in which imagery and words take control in the mind of the artist by force of the fact that he is a master of, or a genius in his vocation. Subjectivity can then largely be discounted. Also psycho-analysis cannot completely explain an artistic work, which represents an evolution by some fresh extension or variation in the existing body of artistic culture, long historically established as the basis on which all artists are free to build new creations, partly incorporating well accepted principles and ideas.

Chapter XI

NARCISSISM

Narcissism is a concept developed by Freud in 1914-1917, and later elaborated. Additional refinements have been added by other psycho-analysts. Initially, it represented a significant modification of psycho-analytical doctrine, but has now become such a settled concept that one finds it hard to believe that narcissism was not part of Freud's original theories of sexuality. It may turn out to be of even greater value than it has already been, both theoretically and therapeutically, and as important as any other of Freud's principal contributions to psycho-analysis.

In Greek art and mythology, Narcissus was the beautiful youth who fell in love with his own image as reflected in a pool, by which he had lingered. The term 'narcissism' appears to have been coined in rather an odd manner in 1898-99. In 1898, in an article on auto-erotism and its psychological aspects, Havelock Ellis had used the expression 'Narcissus-like tendency', and in 1899 in a notice in a German psychiatric journal referring to this article, Dr. Paul Näcke translated the expression as 'Narcismus'. Freud's first reference to 'narcissism' (using of course the German expression) appears to have been in the second edition in 1910 of his study, *Three Essays on the Theory of Sexuality*. But in 1914 there appeared his specific study on the subject, bearing the title, *On Narcissism: An Introduction*. By 1914, as Freud himself acknowledged, the term had been absorbed into the recognized jargon of clinical psychiatric theory.

As psychiatrists first used the term, it signified the attitude of a person who regards his own body as if it were an object of sexuality. There were Narcissus-like cases of individuals experiencing sensual excitement when looking at their own images in mirrors. Freud attached a much wider meaning, more akin to self-love, but capable of embracing these cases of sensual self-infatuation.

But the innovation made by him, and one which must ever remain a mark of his genius, was to use and apply the narcissistic concept in the explanation of much wider theoretical problems than that of the single phenomenon of an individual, sensually self-infatuated to an abnormal degree. These areas include: (a) the historical development of choice of object by the libido; (b) love, in the non-sexual sense; (c) group psychology; (d) the development of the super-ego in some cases; and (e) homosexuality in some of its forms. A most important contribution in this connection was his view that a certain degree of narcissism is possessed by most persons and is normal. This has considerably influenced the theory and therapy of psycho-analysis. It is now commonly accepted by psycho-analysts that some measure of narcissism may be necessary for mental health, and is to be encouraged rather than discouraged. So far as other areas are concerned, psycho-analysts have given attention to the role played or to be played in the neutralization of the destructive drive, and to the question of the narcissistic identification of children with parents, particularly of the boy with the mother. Both areas are of a somewhat technical nature.

Development of object-choice by the libido

Three principles were propounded by Freud in his *Civilization and its Discontents* (published in 1930), as a refinement of his concept of narcissism, namely: (1) the ego itself (i.e. as distinct from other objects) is 'cathected'[1] with libido; (2) the ego is the 'original home' of the libido; and (3) in a certain measure, the ego may continue to be the headquarters of the libido. Remembering that these are propositions applying not merely to the abnormal case of an individual sensually self-infatuated, but to the libidinal development of human beings generally, they serve to clarify his theory regarding the evolution of object-choice by the libido.

The general stages of development, as outlined by Freud, are in their broad sequence as follows:

(a) The auto-erotic stage in early infancy, when there is no question of the ego being the object of libido, but the child's pleasurable sensual feelings are focused on different parts of his

[1] For the meaning of 'cathexis' and 'cathect', see Chapter IV.

body. These include oral and tactile satisfactions. This stage is said to be *object-less.*

(b) The narcissistic or ego-libidinal stage, when the ego becomes the object of the libido. It is a stage of self-love. This may or may not include the libido being directed to certain parts of the body; and in the case of some boys, as direct child observation has proved, there is a feeling of sensual pride in respect to the penis. This feeling may become a matter of fixation, and is said by some analysts to contribute to that unfortunate condition of exhibitionism which brings men into court on charges of obscene behaviour. Another point about this stage of development of object-choice is that the parents often play a role in the intensity of the child's narcissism.[2] So if the father or mother invest the child with love, this may increase the child's narcissism. A reverse situation may occur in which the child receives little or no love, with the result that the child's narcissistic development may be impaired. This latter situation may be crucial for the child's personality, for the low degree or absence of narcissism may prevent movement into the next stage of object-love, and affect future capacity to give or receive love.

(c) The libido, attached to the ego, shifts to some extent from it and is directed to other objects, which may be persons, things (e.g. toys), and animal pets. The parents, and in the case of a boy, the mother become important objects of the child's libido. In the case of the mother and the boy, often a strong identification is established, which, it is claimed with some cogency, may contribute to the subsequent flowering of homosexual tendencies.

(d) The next stage in the sequence of evolution from first object-choices may not be clearly defined, and several possibilities can arise. There may be a reduction in the libido directed to other objects, with a corresponding increase in narcissism of the direct kind, i.e. where the ego itself is the object of libido. Or there may be a more complex development, with libido directed to the ego-ideal, or to some physical aspect such as athletic prowess, or artistic ability. Ideals, norms, and standards may be set up in the mind, by which the person concerned will measure the value of his ego. Of course these ideals, norms, and standards could be of external origin, although eventually incorporated in the personality, and

[2] The role of the mother in giving encouragement to the development of adequate narcissism in the child is stressed by Anna Freud in her study, 'Indications and Contraindications for Child Analysis', *Psychoanalytic Study of the Child,* Vol. XXIII (1968), p. 37, at pp. 40-1.

could contribute to the formation of the ego-ideal. According to Freud, the development proper of the ego occurs, where there is a departure from the earlier narcissism, which he designated as the *primary narcissism*. The departure is brought about by displacement of libido to the ego-ideal, with gratification resulting from the attainment of that ideal. Freud was careful to distinguish this displacement to an ego-ideal from sublimation. The ego-ideal may prompt and influence sublimation, but is not involved in the activity of sublimation itself. This becomes clear if regard is paid to the nature of sublimation, by which the instinctual urges are dechannelled to appropriate goals, without repression, while repression itself is governed by the stringency of the ego-ideal. At the time it was propounded, this concept of primary narcissism was a bold and original theory. While it goes far in explaining many facts of normal development, there still may be special cases where the sequence of evolution of object-choice does not occur in the precise manner postulated by Freud.

However, assessing the evidence in favour of Freud's theory of primary narcissism, one is obliged to admit its weight. There are indications favouring the theory in the data applying to both normal and abnormal persons:

(a) Parents in their over-estimation of their own children show signs of this primary narcissism, because this form of exaggeration is due to the shifting of self-love to objects deemed, in a sense, part of the self.

(b) Many people fall in love[3] with a person, who as Freud said is a narcissistic object-choice, because that person resembles them. Their own selves are adopted as the model for an object-choice. This could not have occurred without the presence of primary narcissism.

(c) According to Freud, in many women maturity results in an intensification of the primary narcissism, and in their case the self-love is so strong that their needs are not so much for loving men, but of being loved. Men who can best meet this requirement are those who will appeal most. This type of narcissistic woman has been depicted time and again with insight by novelists and dramatists.

[3] Note Freud's famous definition of love: 'Being in love is based upon the simultaneous presence of directly sexual tendencies and of sexual tendencies that are inhibited in their aims, so that the object draws a part of the narcissistic ego-libido to itself. It is a condition in which there is only room for the ego and the object'. (See *Group Psychology and the Analysis of the Ego,* 1921, Chapter 12.)

(d) In group psychology, primary narcissism plays a considerable role in forging the bonds that integrate groups, sects, and nations. Where each member of a group is devoted to the same ideals, and respects the same code of behaviour, the narcissistic libido becomes fused with these, and this facilitates the process of identification of one member with other members which is the condition of successful integration. Identification, to which narcissism has contributed, is therefore of considerable sociological significance.

(e) The importance of primary narcissism is also demonstrated in the antagonisms between groups with divergent standards, interests, and views. As Freud has pointed out, narcissism operates towards the self-assertion of individuals, and in the case of differences, members of opposing groups act as if any divergence from their accepted codes and *mores* amounted to a criticism of these lines of development, and a demand for their alteration.

(f) In some individuals, the primary narcissism remains so strong that mistakes and failures are not accepted as such. The rationalization is made either that what was done was correct, or that the failure was due to other persons and to circumstances. This original narcissism may even blind persons to act contrary to self-interest; for example, rejecting the offer of an appointment, considered to be beneath their attainments. Hence self-love and self-interest do not necessarily coincide.

(g) In schizophrenia, as Freud pointed out in 1914, the megalomaniac symptoms consist primarily of a withdrawal of libido from the outer world, and a concentration on the ego, but this total absorbance in the ego is not a new condition, as it must represent an intensification and more obvious manifestation of the original narcissism.

Narcissism and the formation of the super-ego

Freud believed that a contributing factor to the development of the super-ego, that is to say of the ego-ideal component, was a narcissistic process. In a telling description, he said of the ego-ideal that it was the heir to the original narcissism in which the childish ego found its self-sufficiency. This was probably not intended as an absolute proposition, but to cover a great many instances where the narcissistic-ego libido has attached itself to certain ideals and standards that have gradually crystallized into the internalized ego-ideal. This may seem somewhat jargonistic. But what Freud no doubt intended to convey was the ability of the narcissistic libido to move from the ego itself, and become attached to an element or feature connected with the ego. In other instances, it is true, the formation of the super-ego may be due completely to the internalization of parental authority, blended, as claimed by some psycho-analysts, with internalized aggression.

Basic necessity of certain degree of narcissism

As mentioned above, Freud maintained that in a certain measure the ego might continue to be the headquarters of narcissistic libido.

By this, he did not mean that the continuance of narcissism to some extent throughout adulthood was necessarily objectionable or pathological. Psycho-analysts appear to be in agreement that a certain degree of narcissism may contribute to the maintenance of mental health. Originally, in his 1914 study of narcissism, Freud referred to a 'feeling of self-regard' as having a very intimate connection with narcissistic libido, and stated that this feeling appeared to be a measure of the ego. The lowering of narcissistic libido had, in his opinion, a corresponding effect on the feeling of self-regard.

Perhaps today, the expression 'self-regard' would be translatable in the psycho-analytic nomenclature by the term 'normal narcissism', while a lack of self-regard could be rendered as 'absence of normal narcissism'. At all events, it is preferable from the standpoint of psychic health that the narcissistic libido should not be inflexibly directed to ideals and standards of the ego, incapable of achievement by the person concerned. Lapses from norms of excellence can do injury to normal narcissism. It is non-controversial that the feeling of insecurity experienced today by many persons in our urbanized cultures stems from a lowered narcissism, which may exist independently of a severe super-ego and a consequent sense of guilt. The person who states that he is unable to live with himself is an illustration in point. The prevailing social environment in a number of countries today does much to contribute to an unsettling of normal narcissism by the emphasis upon success, and upon the attainment of standards, sometimes beyond the capacity of normal persons.

Paradoxically, narcissism may be reflected in the adoption of postures and attitudes involving some deprivation or suffering, or some curtailment of the ego. For example, some persons may obtain narcissistic gratification from a rigidly ascetic type of existence, upon the ground that this is proof of superiority to other persons.

Narcissism and homosexuality

There is often a close relation between homosexual tendencies and narcissistic tendencies. An intense primary narcissism may govern the choice of object, in the stage of evolution which follows the primary narcissistic phase. There may be a tendency to choose partners as nearly the same as oneself, both in characteristics and in identity of sex. This is often encouraged by environmental factors, including education in schools or colleges which are confined to scholars of the one sex. The strength of the primary narcissism in such persons is shown by the fact that only a portion of their narcissistic libido is diminished by the object-choice of a person of the same sex, and a residue of the narcissistic libido remains, expressed in an intense preoccupation with appearance often found in male persons of homosexual tendencies.

However, this should not be regarded as a general theory of explanation of homosexual urges, but as applying to that special category in which sometimes the object-choice of persons of the same sex has been dictated by the strength of the primary narcissism.

Narcissistic identification with mother; sense of personal identity

The phenomenon of a narcissistic identification of the boy with the mother is one which is frequently found. The attentions of the mother become wrapped up to a considerable degree with the boy's self-love. The attitude of the mother, including her gestures and tenderness, may become essential to the adequacy of his primary narcissism, resulting also in an identification, of varying intensity, with her.[4] This no doubt explains the fact that, in adulthood, some members of the male sex retain in their unconscious this fusion of primary narcissism and of a strong identification with the mother and are unable to form a genuine hetero-sexual relationship.

The relationship in infancy with the mother and the original

[4] See Anna Freud's study, 'Indications and Contraindications for Child Analysis', *Psychoanalytic Study of the Child,* Vol. XXIII (1968), p. 37, at pp. 40-1, where it is also emphasised that encouragement from the mother is needed for the development of the boy's cognitive functions, and of his masculinity.

narcissism appear to be also important for the emergence of a sense of identity. The support of the mother, even before there is a transition from the purely auto-erotic stage into the primary narcissistic stage, may be decisive in imparting the first necessary sense of identity to child. It is possible to argue that the phase of primary narcissism depends upon the child having acquired such a sense of identity, and that the presence of narcissistic libido serves to maintain and strengthen this sense of identity. If this hypothesis were correct, some clinical cases of disturbance of a sense of identity could well be due to a lowering of narcissism. An even wider proposition may be ventured, namely that this close relationship between the existence of primary narcissism and the emergence and maintenance of a sense of personal identity may be fundamental to a proper understanding of the nature and functions of narcissism in general.[5]

In the preceding chapter we have referred to Freud's explanation that the smile on Mona Lisa's face was a kind of reproduction of the memory retained by Leonardo of his mother's gestures in earliest childhood. Perhaps there was more than this; there may well have been in Leonardo a narcissistic identification with his mother, crucial also for what we call today a sense of personal identity. We have already referred to the tendency of artists, generally unconscious, to strengthen by artistic creation a sense of identity which is subject to disturbance.

The narcissistic personality

The degree of narcissism varies from person to person, and appears to depend to some extent on the particular social culture of the community to which the individual concerned belongs.

A high degree of narcissism in women, reflected in such matters as fashion, cosmetics and hair-styling, is now in accordance with most cultures. In earlier centuries, a somewhat similar position applied to men, but the Victorian age is said by some authors to have altered this. Exhibitions in museums showing men's attire in the nineteenth century do not, however, suggest that men ceased to be preoccupied with dress, and with the styling of their hair,

5 For a valuable, penetrating article on the relationship between narcissism and sense of identity, and which emphasizes the fundamental importance of Freud's theory of narcissism, because of its bearing on identity, see H. Lichtenstein, 'The Role of Narcissism in the Emergence and Maintenance of a Primary Identity', *International Journal of Psycho-Analysis,* Vol. 45 (1964), pp. 49-56.

moustaches, and beards. In certain academic and professional circles, a high level of male narcissism continues to be expressed in the wearing of ritualistic or quasi-sacerdotal robes, gowns, wigs, and headgear for particular ceremonies or in the normal course of duty.

Thus it cannot be said that a high degree of narcissism is necessarily abnormal, nor can it be maintained that it is pathological. It is only to be comdemned insofar as the highly narcissistic person yields to his narcissism by false rationalizations or actions contrary to self-interest.

All highly narcissistic persons are nevertheless not necessarily free of feelings of insecurity. In some individuals a high level of narcissism may coexist with a severe super-ego, rendering him subject to self-critical tendencies. This is generally because the narcissism attaches itself to personal traits and characteristics not condemned by the super-ego. The relationship between secondary narcissism and the super-ego can, in the case of certain individuals, be rather complex.

General

It should not be thought that some psycho-analysts do not dispute certain of Freud's propositions and the implications flowing from his theory.

While the theory is considered to be of clinical value for the understanding of personality and to have made a significant contribution to the methodology of psycho-analysis, some doubts have persisted concerning its universal applicability and concerning the terms in which it was formulated. The concept of a primary narcissism has been queried, because it is claimed that this may have been preceded in the earliest stages of infancy by a primary love of the mother, which may be at the root of what Freud described as primary narcissism. There are some doubts also as to whether there is at a later stage in childhood in all cases, an oscillation backwards and forwards of ego-libido into object-libido, and *vice versa*. Above all, the hypothesis has been propounded that narcissism does not represent a libidinal cathexis of the ego, but of the self (see Chapter III). This hypothesis cannot in any strict sense be reconciled with the theory of narcissism as formulated by Freud, and as it has been further elaborated.

Under these circumstances, it is perhaps trite to say that the last word on narcissism has not yet been said by the exponents of psycho-analytic doctrine.

Chapter XII

INFLUENCE OF PSYCHO-ANALYSIS

It cannot be said that psycho-analysts have been indifferent to the impact upon human thought of psycho-analytical doctrine.[1] But naturally as experience has taught them, there is some difficulty of communication with those who are unsympathetic towards psycho-analysis. Thus, it has more usually fallen to non-analysts to define and measure the extent to which psycho-analysis has exercised influence.[2] Contrary to general belief, psycho-analysts have not purported to be evangelists, supporting a new gospel concerning the human mind. They have not been oblivious to a persistent hostility towards psycho-analytical doctrine, ever manifesting itself in new and different forms.

Freud always recognized that if resistances were encountered from patients actually seeking to be cured of nervous or emotional disorders, it was only to be expected that the theories of psycho-analysis would meet with much stronger, more widespread resistances from people who felt neither the need nor the desire for analytical therapy. Accordingly, the opposition to psycho-analysis did not surprise or disappoint him.

Leaving aside such antagonism, it is the object of the present

[1] Thus psycho-analysts have frequently participated in interdisciplinary symposia or discussions concerned with the impact of psycho-analysis upon scientific thought, philosophy, art, law, and other humanistic disciplines. E.g., the symposium at New York in March 1958 on the scientific status of psycho-analysis, the papers of which are published in Sidney Hook (ed.), *Psychoanalysis* . . . .

[2] See, e.g., the distinguished study, *Freud,* London 1971, by Professor Richard Wollheim, Professor of the Philosophy of Mind and Logic in London University.

chapter to assess briefly what influence psycho-analysis has had upon the fields of philosophy, sociology and human culture, or literature.

Influence of psycho-analysis upon philosophy

The influence of psycho-analysis has been imperceptible on certain philosophers. However, it is believed that this is not due to any discrimination against psycho-analysis as such, but to a certain measure of indifference to scientific advances in the fields of psychology, physiology, and neurology, and a preference for the traditional tools of philosophic thought.

On another level, there are the philosophers who have been critical of psycho-analysis considered not as a scientific discipline in its own right but as a branch of knowledge within a philosophic frame of reference. In other words, psycho-analysis has been treated as if its exponents were advancing a self-contained philosophic system, as if concepts such as the unconscious, repression, and sublimation, for example, were propounded as philosophic abstractions. Hence, there is the inevitable criticism by such philosophers that the methodology of psycho-analysis is weak, that the validation of its hypotheses leaves much to be desired, and that the reasoning is mainly *ex post facto* and based upon an inadequate body of data. Considered from this standpoint, the criticism is of cogency. Psycho-analysts themselves would agree that the methodology of psycho-analytic doctrine needs to be improved. But does that negate all the value of its propositions so far as they bear upon the problems of philosophy? Moreover, it can well be said that the methodology of most, if not all, humanistic sciences requires improvement.

It is true, nevertheless, that psycho-analysis cannot supply the answer to many of the key problems of philosophy, although it may provide a new kind of perspective for examining them.[3]

For such a perspective to be acquired by philosophers, it is necessary that they become cognisant of the 'vast amount of empirical detail garnered by psychoanalysts in the last half-century as well as the complexity of many of the theoretical concepts employed in psychoanalysis'.[4] Even though these theoretical concepts cannot

[3] Dr Heinz Hartmann in Sidney Hook (ed.), *Psychoanalysis . . .* , p. 3. But see in the same volume Donald Williams, 'Philosophy and Psychoanalysis', pp. 133-56.

[4] John Hospers, 'Philosophy and Psychoanalysis' in Sidney Hook (ed.), *Psychoanalysis . . .* , p. 336. See also Morris Lazerowitz, 'The Relevance of Psychoanalysis to Psychiatry', ibid., pp. 133-56.

be 'neatly pinpointed and encapsulated in one simple formula', and are difficult to master because of their richness and complexity, they are 'workable ones and are used again and again every day by practising psychoanalysts.'[5]

Yet a number of philosophers have been sympathetic towards certain concepts and theories of psycho-analysis, while entertaining reservations about other parts of psycho-analytic doctrine. There are few philosophers prepared to be sympathetic towards psycho-analysis taken as a whole. The following are the points, among others, in psycho-analytical doctrine which have made some impression, and have not been treated with unreserved scepticism:

(a) The endeavour to give a scientific explanation of the working of the unconscious, the conception of the unconscious as dynamic in operation, and the influence of the unconscious as conditioning behaviour through hidden motivations. Psycho-analysis has also been regarded as contributing much to philosophic thought by breaking down the barriers between the conscious and the unconscious.

(b) The notion both expressed and implied in psycho-analytical doctrine of the continuity of body and mind. Freud always remained insistent that the concepts and hypotheses advanced by him would at some time in the future become capable of expression in neurological or physiological terms. The continuity of body and mind is manifested most clearly in the psycho-analytical theories regarding the development of sexuality and of its component drives, and in respect to anxiety and hysteria.

(c) The close relation between thought and emotion, on the one hand, and action or behaviour, on the other. This connection comes out most clearly in the psycho-analytical theory concerning symptoms and inhibitions, and in regard to the obsessional neuroses.

(d) The absence of any sharp line of division between normality and abnormality, so far as concerns the psyches of human beings. According to psycho-analytical theory, a pathological mental condition represents an intensification of normal tendencies, or in the case of conflict producing a neurotic condition, some difference in the quantitative factor as between that condition and a non-neurotic condition. In other words, from the philosophic standpoint, the abnormal mind does not have to be considered as exceptional, and standing apart from the normal mind.

(e) The structural theory of the mind, with its division into the

[5] John Hospers, 'Philosophy and Psychoanalysis', p. 344.

ego, the id, and the super-ego, each a group of functions, expresses primarily a conationalist conception of the mind—constantly striving, with the ego, the id, and the super-ego directed towards their respective goals. In other words, the mind is not to be conceived as primarily cognitive and abstractly passive.

(f) The concept of psychic determinism as conditioning human attitudes and human behaviour. Some philosophers have regarded psychic determinism as specially significant insofar as it has clarified the processes in such seemingly meaningless or inexplicably accidental phenomena as slips of the tongue and pen, lapses of memory, and 'symptomatic acts'. Also considered impressive is the application of the deterministic method to interpret dreams, and explain the hidden meaning of myths and legends. There has been some philosophic criticism of the psycho-analytical emphasis on mental determinism as being 'fatalistic'. It is difficult to see how this criticism can apply to the mere interpretation of past phenomena such as dreams, slips of the tongue, and long standing myths, while in regard to human behaviour generally, it overlooks the fact that psycho-analysts generally envision a future state of affairs in which the human species will be able to control consciously the unconscious forces of the mind.

(g) The importance of experiences in early childhood as conditioning future behaviour. This is not accepted by philosophers without some reservations.

To the extent of this acceptance by *some* philosophers only of *some* parts of psycho-analytical doctrine as being of philosophic value, it can be said that psycho-analysis has had an influence on contemporary philosophy. But, with a few exceptions, there continues to be strong resistance by philosophers to the fundamental concepts of repression, sublimation, and the death instinct; this is on various grounds, mainly that these result in logical contradictions with other theories and concepts of psycho-analysis, or involve pure assumptions, or do not have as wide a scope as suggested.

Misunderstandings by philosophers of basic psycho-analytical theories nevertheless continue, and reflect the difficulty of smooth interplay between philosophy and psycho-analytic doctrine. One of the most misunderstood theories is that of the structure of personality as consisting of the ego, the id, and the super-ego (see Chapter III). These three divisions of personality are sometimes misconceived by philosophers as being mental 'entities', while it is not fully appreciated that psycho-analysts consider these as interacting, with such interaction giving rise to conflicts between inconsistent tendencies. Nor has due regard been paid to post-1939 developments in psycho-analytic ego psychology.

Another misconception of some philosophers is that psycho-analysis involves passive acceptance of the irrationality of mankind. This is somewhat akin to the idea that the psychic determinism applied in psycho-analytical doctrine is 'fatalistic'. Such an approach overlooks the very rationalism of psycho-analysis, reflected in a method of investigation based on the principle that mental processes can be subjected to rational scientific examination, and to rational guidance and direction. The psycho-analytic movement can indeed be characterized as largely one of rational humanism. The ultimate, but far distant objective is that one day rationality will assume control over the unconscious forces that tend towards the destruction of the human species.

Influence of psycho-analysis on sociology and human culture

It would not be disputed that the influence of psycho-analysis upon sociological thought has been more marked than its impact upon philosophy. Sociology seems to have almost gratefully taken over certain of the concepts first developed within the folds of psycho-analytic doctrine, such as cathexis, identification, projection, sublimation, and libido. There is, also, considerable sympathy among sociologists for the structural theory of personality, as a composite of the ego, the id, and the super-ego.

Beyond that, there are natural limitations in the application of psycho-analysis to sociology. Psycho-analysis does not supply sufficient tools to assist in developing sociological knowledge.[6] It can do no more than make a contribution in specific areas, or provide additional insights for the understanding of particular problems. For instance, Freud's classical book, *Group Psychology and the Analysis of the Ego* (1921), has done much for the investigation of group processes by showing that one of the integrating factors in the evolution of groups is that of identification by members of the particular group with each other or with some common ideal. Also, with regard to cultures, psycho-analysis has demonstrated how in the context of repression, a culture may be developed through the process of sublimation, and transmitted to later generations by virtue of the fact that the super-ego formed in children

[6] See A. Inkeles, 'Psychoanalysis and Sociology' in Sidney Hook (ed.), *Psychoanalysis . . .* , pp. 117-29.

impels them both in childhood and later in adulthood to conform. The influence of the social environment in producing frustration, and the reaction of aggression has been dealt with by some writers. The sociological concept of rationality, in the sense of goal-directed behaviour, can be illuminated through psycho-analytic ego psychology, indicating that the seat of rationality is in the ego, although there is a danger of a role being played by the defence mechanisms such as rationalization and undoing (see Chapter III). Psycho-analysis can also to some extent elucidate certain of the unconscious factors conditioning socially deviant behaviour, and protest movements. In some instances, this resistance to authority has its roots in the Oedipus complex (see Chapters III and IV).

Nor can one overlook the revolutionary effect on Western cultures and *mores* generated as a result of psycho-analytic theories concerning repression, sexuality, and sublimation. It is true that this came about partly because of two fundamental misunderstandings among the public of what Freud meant by repression and sexuality. In respect to repression, this was erroneously taken to signify frustration, purely and simply. Inasmuch as psycho-analysis had demonstrated that the repression of instinctual urges could cause anxiety and neurotic illness in the case of certain persons, people leapt to the conclusion that the frustration of sex was in all cases fundamentally bad from the standpoint of mental health. In regard to sexuality, it was assumed that Freud's references to the sexual instinct meant sexual intercourse and its immediate preliminaries, instead of the wide meaning of sensual urges and sensual energy which he in fact attributed to that instinct.

In addition, Freud's theory that many human activities constituted sublimations of the erotic drive contributed towards a more enlightened attitude towards sexuality. Leaving aside those who took umbrage at the idea that much of human culture was due to a de-channelling of sexuality towards de-sexualized aims, the theory of sublimation served to demonstrate the normality and importance of the sexual instinct. Indeed wider inferences could be drawn. If human culture depended in so material a measure upon the sublimation of the erotic urge, how was it possible to disparage sexuality as merely part of the lower, animal-like impulses of the human species?

The influence of psycho-analysis upon human culture has not been confined to the removal of shams and self-deceptions concerning sexuality. It covers a much broader field. Freud's emphasis on the importance of the early years of childhood in shaping character, and in producing repressions leading to neurosis, as well as on the significance of maternal love, ultimately contributed to the development of child analysis and to research and inquiries by way of direct child observation. The consequence was that his hypotheses were confirmed. This resulted in attention being given to the early rearing of children, and to stress being placed upon the vital aspect of maternal care in early infancy, and upon the child's need for the mother's love.[7] Indirectly, Freud's theories had an impact upon the whole attitude of society and of the courts towards the adoption of illegitimate children, and in divorce and other matrimonial proceedings towards the question of custody orders, with a leaning towards the wife, where the child was in the early years of infancy, and dependent upon the mother and her love. There are traces of the influence of Freud's theories concerning maternal love and the importance of the period of early infancy to be found in some of the terms of the Declaration of the Rights of the Child, adopted by the General Assembly of the United Nations on 20 November, 1959.

The present trend towards some form of imparting sexual knowledge to children in the early years, as a means of avoiding repression or the appearance in adulthood of immature sexual fixations, can be traced to the influence of psycho-analytic doctrine. It may be recalled that as long ago as 1907 Freud was the author of a remarkable open letter on the sexual enlightenment of children.[8]

These represent only some of the varied contributions of psycho-analysis to sociological thought and human culture. Psycho-analysis is after all no more than a part of that wide discipline now known as study of man, and it cannot solve all the problems of civilization which come within the range of that discipline, nor is that the purpose of psycho-analysis. Within a limited frame of reference, psycho-analytic doctrine can contribute towards elucidating the nature of those unconscious forces in the mind which need to be controlled if civilization is to survive. Moreover, one can hope that Freud's warning against over-straining sublimations in the interests of a more highly developed and more refined social culture will be heeded.

[7] For an acknowledgement of the contribution made by psycho-analysis in this connection, see John Bowlby, *Child Care and the Growth of Love,* 2nd edn. 1965, p. 16.

[8] See *Freud: On War, Sex and Neurosis,* New York 1947, pp. 149-57, for the text of an English translation of this letter.

Influence of psycho-analysis on literature

It remains to deal briefly with the influence of psycho-analysis upon literature. Such influence has been, and is now more than ever, manifest in the novel, drama, poetry, biography, and literary criticism. The most usually given illustration of this influence is the 'stream-of-consciousness' technique—comparable to free associations by a subject under analysis—employed in novels. In addition there has been the theme of unconscious motivations for human behaviour of an irrational nature. In many instances, knowledge of psycho-analytic doctrine has sharpened the perception with which the novelist has presented his theme.

The influence is also marked in the case of drama. To take one example, plays have time and again presented the theme of family conflict, as affected, in the case of members of the family, by unconscious motivations, and by a disturbance of a sense of identity. It is true, however, that one can often discern an artificial intention to conform to what is assumed to be psycho-analytic doctrine, with the playwright sometimes misconstruing or misconceiving the precise applicability of psycho-analytic concepts and hypotheses. Another point is that often no awareness is shown of post-1939 developments in psycho-analysis.

The same observations apply to biography and literary criticism, where frequently the author searches for the unconscious basis governing the career or literary products of his subject. Apart from such psycho-analytic assessments forming part only of a biographical or literary study, there have been instances of studies, wholly and exclusively of the nature of a psycho-analytic summation of the personality characteristics of biographical personages.[9] The difficulties involved in making such a psycho-analytic personality study are obvious, and include such matters as the unavailability of important data concerning the subject's life, the fact that the materials, although they may consist of such significant items as letters and records of conversations, are not products of free association as would occur in a clinical analysis, and the problems

[9] Examples, in the case of Freud himself, are the classical study of Leonardo da Vinci, published in 1910 (see Chapters X and XI), and the more controversial book, W. C. Bullitt and S. Freud, *Thomas Woodrow Wilson: A Psychological Study,* Boston 1966. For a psycho-analytical study in respect to John Keats, see James W. Hamilton, 'Object Loss, Dreaming and Creativity: The Poetry of John Keats', *Psychoanalytic Study of the Child,* Vol. XXIV (1969), pp. 488-531.

of interpretation where gaps and inconsistencies exist.[10] Thus, however cogent such assessments may be, one must treat them with a certain reserve. That such psycho-analytic studies continue to be made, the difficulties mentioned notwithstanding, is proof that the influence of psycho-analysis is not waning.

[10] See John E. Mack, 'Psychoanalysis and Historical Biography', *Journal of the American Psychoanalytic Association,* Vol. 19 (1971), p. 143 at pp. 173, 178-9.

Chapter XIII

PSYCHO-ANALYSIS AND THE LAW

The relevance of psycho-analysis to legal issues, and the legal implications of psycho-analysis may be considered under three broad headings, of the nature of queries: (1) to what extent does psycho-analysis, either by itself or in conjunction with modern general psychiatry, have impact upon the traditional assumptions of the law concerning the nature of the human mind and of human personality; (2) has psycho-analysis contributed any additional knowledge as to the mind and personality which could assist in the better, or more precise formulation of legal rules, or in the more effective administration of the law; and (3) what special insights can psycho-analysis provide for the purpose of clarifying the nature of the law, and of legal institutions? The matter will be dealt with under each of these queries in turn.[1]

[1] For books and studies on the subject, see the following: Albert A. Ehrenzweig, *Psychoanalytic Jurisprudence* on ethics, aesthetics and law . . . on crimes, tort, and procedure, Leyden 1971; 'A Psychoanalysis of the Insanity Plea—Clues to the Problem of Criminal Responsibility and Insanity in the Death Cell', *Yale Law Journal,* Vol. 73 (1963-1964), pp. 425-41, and 'Psychoanalytic Jurisprudence: A Common Language for Babylon', *Columbia Law Review,* Vol. 65 (1965), pp. 1331-1360; L. V. Kaplan 'An Academic Lawyer Plays Armchair Analyst: Some Speculations on the Relevance of Psychoanalysis to the Law', *Nebraska Law Review,* Vol. 46 (1967), pp. 759-97; Joseph Goldstein, 'Psychoanalysis and Jurisprudence', *Yale Law Journal,* Vol. 77 (1967-1968), pp. 1053-77; Alan M. Dershowitz, 'Psychiatry in the Legal Process: "A Knife that cuts both ways" ', in A. E. Sunderland (ed.), *The Path of the Law from 1967* (1968), pp. 71-84; R. Bienenfeld, 'Prolegomena to a Psychoanalysis of Law and Justice', *California Law Review,* Vol. 53 (1965), pp. 957-1028, and 1254-336; A. Katz, 'A Psycho-Analytic Peek at Conspiracy', *Buffalo Law Review,* Vol. 20 (1970), pp. 239-51.

(1) Impact of psycho-analysis upon legal assumptions

The principal traditional assumptions of the law concerning the nature of mind and personality, which run counter to the basic teachings of psycho-analysis, are as follows.

(A) The law looks upon the mind as a *conscious* entity which, in the normal condition, is largely rational, and in the abnormal condition, largely irrational. For instance, this approach is reflected in the legal rules dealing with intention as an element of criminal or tortious liability, intention being conceived as a conscious experience of the mind. This conception of a conscious mind only is of course in conflict with the fundamental psycho-analytic postulates of the division of the human psyche into the conscious and the unconscious, and of the dynamic role of the unconscious in motivating irrational behaviour. It is clear from these psycho-analytic postulates that: (i) certain legal rules may need to be reformulated so as to encompass both conscious behaviour and behaviour which is unconsciously motivated; and (ii) due regard must be paid to these postulates in the application and administration of the law.

Point (i) may be illustrated by section 2 of the English Homicide Act 1957, dealing with the circumstances under which mental disorder may be relied upon as a defence to a murder charge, and applying the principle of diminished responsibility. The rules in section 2 replaced the *M'Naghten rules* (see Appendix III) under which the defence of insanity to a murder charge was open only if the accused 'was labouring under such a defect of reason, from disease of the mind, as not to know the nature and quality of the act he was doing, or, if he did know it, that he did not know he was doing what was wrong'. That is to say the test was based on conscious knowledge of right and wrong. Section 2 allows a defence based upon 'abnormality of mind'; the defendant at the time of the murder must have been 'suffering from such abnormality of mind (whether arising from a condition of arrested or retarded development of mind or any inherent causes or induced by disease or injury) as substantially impaired his mental responsibility for his acts and omissions in doing or being a party to the killing'. Thus the new test can embrace both mental abnormality of a conscious character, and mental abnormality springing from unconscious causes.[2]

The need to have regard to psycho-analytic theories of the

[2] The case of *Attorney-General for the State of South Australia v. Brown,* (1960) A.C. 432 (Privy Council) illustrates the difference in this respect between section 2 and the *M'Naghten* rules.

unconscious in applying or administering the law may be illustrated by cases relating to testamentary incapacity, or involving applications under the Testator's Family Maintenance legislation, where no adequate provision has been made by a testator for the prescribed members of his family. Frequently, it will be found that the testator has acted irrationally, although not suffering from any pronounced mental disorder, and that the explanation lies in unconscious factors, such as unconscious aggressivity directed against his children, or—in an extreme case—an irrational belief, conditioned by unconscious factors, that he is being persecuted by his family. In such instances, an unconsciously motivated irrational intention, as expressed in the testator's will, ought not, as a general rule, to be given full effect by the courts.[3]

(B) The law still makes no distinction between the psychoses and the neuroses in its treatment of the subject of mental disorder, although such a distinction is not only a commonplace of psycho-analytic doctrine, but of modern general psychiatry. It is clear that in several areas, for example legislation concerned with mental health, or with legal incapacity and the protection of the person affected by mental illness, the distinction should be made. The psychotic is remote from reality whereas the neurotic, as Freud has pointed out, continues to retain some dependence upon reality.

(C) The law continues to make a sharp division between normality and abnormality, so far as mental health is concerned. The expression 'abnormality of mind' is in fact used in section 2 of the English Homicide Act, 1957. It is basic to psycho-analytic doctrine that there is no sharp differentiation between mental normality and psychiatric disorder, and that the mental dynamics are the same in all cases, except that differences of degree in such matters as conflicts between the ego and the super-ego, and between the ego and the id, may result in illness. The expression 'abnormality of mind' in the Act has already caused difficulty in its interpretation, which could have been avoided had the expression 'psychiatric disorder' simply been used.[4]

[3] As in the case of *Derrett v. Hall* (unreported, High Court of Australia, 4 February 1942), referred to by Williams, J., in *Bull v. Fulton* (1942), 66 C.L.R. 295, at p. 339.

[4] Under these circumstances, Lord Parker, C.J., cannot altogether be blamed for explaining the expression 'abnormality of mind' in these tautologous words: '"Abnormality of mind"... means a state of mind so different from that of ordinary human beings that the reasonable man would term it abnormal'. See his judgment in *Regina v. Byrne* (1960) 2 Q.B. 396, at p. 403.

(D) The law is still governed by an unreasonably severe approach towards the sexual deviances and towards allegedly pornographic art and literature. Psycho-analytic doctrine has contributed largely to an explanation of the origins of the sexual perversions, which are shown to be attributable to early childhood, and in some instances to be due to disturbances of the mother-infant relationship or failures in development, also in childhood. In particular, the penalties assigned for such sexual offences as genital exhibitionism, whether of males to males or of males to females, are savage in the extreme. This can be partly accounted for, under psycho-analytic doctrine, by the fact that in most people the tendencies to sexual deviance are present in the unconscious, but are repressed, by virtue of the super-ego; partly by the process of projection, the super-ego vents its aggressivity upon other persons who would indulge overtly in the sexual deviances. Similar considerations apply to the catch-phrase 'standards of the community', which is usually invoked as the criterion of obscenity in prosecutions for the publication or distribution of pornographic materials. The 'standards' are to a large extent a reflection of a reaction against repressed sexuality due to the influence of the super-ego, and do not represent a rational, unemotional attitude towards the sexual instinct. In addition, so far as the sexual deviances are concerned, it has been shown that in some instances the law is marred by false assumptions about particular deviances. For example, it may assume that, as a general rule, a person guilty of exhibitionism alone is likely to develop into a dangerous sex offender, capable of sexual assaults, yet this is untrue.[5]

(E) The courts, and to a lesser extent the legislature, continue to regard a symptom such as a delusion or irrational belief as a disease by which the personality has been afflicted, rather than as an expression of some wider causes, lying deep in the unconscious. In the past, courts have proceeded to deal with cases involving evidence of delusions or irrational beliefs without the assistance of medical evidence.[6] But in view of the non-controversial psycho-analytic and psychiatric truth that a symptom requires explanation in the light of the whole personality, either legislation should

5 See Morse, in *Tulane Law Review,* Vol. 42 (1967-1968), pp. 122-5.

6 As in the case of *Timbury v. Coffee,* 66 C.L.R. (1941), p. 277, at p. 282. The case is notable for the statement by Dixon, J., at p. 284: 'We are not bound to go on applying views held over a century ago about mental disturbance and insanity and to disregard modern knowledge and understanding of such conditions'.

provide that courts be assisted in such cases by the testimony of psychiatrists or, as a rule of practice, courts should insist upon such testimony being made available to them.

(F) Legislation dealing with the subject of mental health and the treatment of psychiatric disorders continues to be based upon the assumption that only a small minority of the population need come within the range of the statutory provisions on the subject. This assumption is in conflict with what may be inferred from psycho-analytic experience, taken in conjunction with other evidence, such as the number of persons who have recourse to marriage guidance counselling services, rejections on medical grounds of recruits for the armed services, and the numerous patients of general practitioners who are treated for nervous ailments. The need for a nation-wide attack upon the problem of mental and neurotic disorders cannot really be gainsaid. Coupled with such a wider legislative framework, there should ideally be steps taken to institute the training of psycho-analysts and psychiatrists upon a national basis, and to stimulate and finance research upon similar lines.

(G) The courts and lawyers adhere to a number of erroneous assumptions concerning the deterrent effect of penalties for certain offences, and concerning the possibilities of the rehabilitation of offenders. In regard to penalties, this may be illustrated by the current impression that stiffer penalties than usual will be effective to curb 'protest' movements, such as student protest demonstrations. Professor Joseph Goldstein has pointed out[7] that far from having this effect, psycho-analytic insights reveal that a severe repressive action by the criminal law against mass demonstrators will serve rather as an invitation to regress to a primitive level of the mind, with a suspension of rational judgment, and to produce riotous and violent behaviour, so that the deterrent effect of the penalties is lost. In the matter of rehabilitation of offenders, courts are sometimes induced to act upon too optimistic an assessment of the possibilities of psychiatric treatment of offenders, especially in cases where the delinquent behaviour is conditioned by deeply embedded unconscious factors, with strong resistances to treatment. Psycho-analytic experience shows not only that such cases usually require lengthy, protracted therapy, but that one must be sceptical about a favourable outcome.

[7] See Joseph Goldstein, 'On the Function of Criminal Law in Riot Control', *Psychoanalytic Study of the Child,* Vol. XXIV (1969), p. 463, at p. 484.

(2) Contribution of additional knowledge by psycho-analysis

The contribution of additional knowledge by psycho-analysis, to assist in the better formulation of legal rules, or in the more effective administration of the law, may be illustrated by a number of examples.

First, with reference to the law of child custody, there are the advances in knowledge, largely due to psycho-analytic doctrine and experience, in the area of the psychological development of young children, and of the mother-child relationship in infancy. Early maternal deprivation has been shown to be a significant factor in causing later personality disturbances, whereas the continuation of the affection of the mother or a mother-figure without interruption can influence the growth of a secure personality, without development failure.[8] Moreover, as Anna Freud has pointed out,[9] in the case of boys, maternal encouragement and influence may be necessary for the boy's proper development into masculine adulthood. These considerations appear to make it imperative that, in the absence of evidence of disturbance in the mother-infant relationship or of serious mental instability of the mother, the court should be bound to order that the custody of children under the age of five years be with the mother. It is maintained[10] that, in addition, the court should have the assistance of psychiatric testimony concerning the mental condition of each of the parents.

Second, through psycho-analysis much has been learned regarding the factors which can lead to a marriage breakdown, particularly factors involved in sexual incompatibility or disharmony so far as these are of psychic origin. Psychic impotence was identified by Freud as due to an arrest occurring during the course of the development of the libido towards a normal form. The arrest may be caused by an unconscious form of incest prohibition, linked to a strong identification with the mother, or be influenced by some instability in the boy's relationship with his mother, such as a lack of encouragement in the development of his masculinity. Identification with parents can affect not merely psychic potency, but operate as a disturbing factor in the normal relations between

[8] See H. A. Finlay and Stanley Gold, 'The Paramount Interest of the Child in Law and Psychiatry', *Australian Law Journal,* Vol. 45 (1971), p. 82 at pp. 92-3.

[9] 'Indications and Contraindications for Child Analysis', *Psychoanalytic Study of the Child,* Vol. XXIII (1968), p. 37 at pp. 40-1.

[10] H. A. Finlay and Stanley Gold, in *Australian Law Journal,* Vol. 45 (1971), p. 94.

married people. Ideally, this new knowledge regarding the causes of marriage breakdowns should have opened the way for psychiatric evidence to be admitted to prove either impossibility of reinstating the marriage, or that there was some chance of reconciliation. However, such knowledge has to compete with other values involved in the institution of marriage. Hence, it has to be related to one of the set 'grounds' of dissolution of marriage such as cruelty. These do not include marriage breakdown or sexual incompatibility.

A third and final example concerns the question of the credibility of witnesses. Freud's *The Psychopathology of Everyday Life* showed how the unconscious mind can operate so as to produce forgetfulness and lapses of memory as well as false readings and distortions of vision. His propositions concerning the unconscious mechanisms which result in temporary forgetfulness or visual distortions have become largely non-controversial. Yet for all practical purposes these are outside the knowledge of judges or of advocates practising in the courts, notwithstanding that they have an important bearing upon the credibility of witnesses. For instance, the inability of a witness to recall a particular name or some particular fact, due to such unconscious factors as were identified by Freud, ought not to be considered as rendering the whole of his testimony unreliable. It should be possible for counsel to explain this lapse of memory on the ground mentioned, while judges should equally be alert to this, in order that the evidence of a witness should not be wholly discounted.

(3) Psycho-analytic insights into the nature of legal institutions

The fact that psycho-analysis can offer special insights into the nature of law and of legal institutions can best be illustrated by the position of the Crown in the legal systems of Australia and of the United Kingdom. In theory, the Crown is the source and fount of all law. Legislation requires the assent of the Crown or the Crown's representative, criminal prosecutions are instituted in the name of the Crown, and prosecutors are said to appear for the Crown. All this is purely symbolic, theoretical, and abstract, for as everyone knows, it is the government which actually rules. Yet this formal position of the Crown as the head of the legal system serves to uphold respect for, and to maintain the sanctity of the law, because it harmonizes with certain characteristic concepts in the unconscious of members of the public.

First, there is the symbolism involved in the nature of the Crown.

It corresponds to the monarch or sovereign, who, for the unconscious, stands as a symbol for the father. Second, we have the duality of Crown and government, the former traditionally above reproach, the latter liable to change and displacement. The unconscious ambivalent attitude towards a father, and therefore towards authority, is adequately satisfied. The aggressive, and if necessary, destructive feelings involved in the repressed Oedipal complex can be directed against the government so that the Crown is shielded from such display of aggressivity. Being symbolic and formal only, it is sacrosanct and a proper object for the cathexis of the feelings of love and respect which are part of the unconscious ambivalent attitude towards the father.

The result is that the authority of the law harmonizes with the deepest unconscious feelings of the majority of citizens. It may seem illogical and unreal that this effect is secured through the device of an abstract symbol such as the Crown, but that only serves to underscore the importance of symbolism for the unconscious mind according to psycho-analytic doctrine.

Appendix I

SHORT HISTORICAL SUMMARY OF DEVELOPMENT OF PSYCHO-ANALYSIS

A short historical survey of the development of psycho-analysis must necessarily be confined to the principal events and to the broad trends. Apart from other matters to be dealt with, a full account would require a detailed country-by-country survey, which is beyond the scope of the present book. The growth of psycho-analysis may be considered in three periods: (1) from about 1882 to 1910; (2) from 1910 to 1939 and (3) from 1939 to the present.

(1) Period 1882-1910

While Sigmund Freud was a student, still occupied with final medical examinations in Vienna, Dr Joseph Breuer (1842-1925), a Viennese physician, had in the period 1880-1882 been experimenting with a method of treating a patient suffering from hysteria. Dr Breuer ascertained that pathogenic hysterical symptoms might be made to disappear or lose their intensity if, under hypnosis, the patient could be brought to remember certain past emotional situations and the associated feelings, and to talk about these. The process of speaking about these painful, emotionally tinged memories of a somewhat buried nature, enabled the patient to ventilate or discharge, to some extent, the inner tensions involved. Freud had become friendly with Breuer who, in November 1882, gave an account of the treatment to Freud, whose main interest then was in research in neuro-physiology. The disclosure made an impression upon him.

In 1885 Freud left for Paris where he entered upon studies under Charcot (1825-1893), the distinguished French neurologist. He was able at close hand to observe Charcot's methods of treating hysteria and other psychopathological conditions, including hypnosis, and to obtain some insight into the tenor of Charcot's approach to the investigation of hysterical symptoms. Charcot undoubtedly had considerable influence on Freud, to the extent of even inspiring him throughout his subsequent career.[1] Yet Freud perceived Charcot's scientific limitations,[2] one being, as he was to point out in his American lectures of 1909, that Charcot had no natural bent for deducing psychological theories. Freud however possessed this talent, which had been fortified by his research in neuro-physiology. In fact, Freud actually gave an account to Charcot of Breuer's disclosures concerning his treatment of the hysterical patient, but Charcot did not react with any interest. One matter worth mentioning is that during Freud's stay in Paris, Charcot appears to have confided in him that sexual difficulties lay at the root of most ailments treated by him, a remark which apparently left some impression upon Freud.[3]

Upon returning to Vienna in 1886, Freud began to practise in nervous diseases, including hysteria, thus giving up his research in neuro-physiology. This decision may well be attributed to the effect of studying under Charcot.[4] Freud had given some account to Breuer of what he had seen in Paris, and he became associated with Breuer in the investigation of cases of hysteria. Reference should also be made to the fact that in 1889, in the course of a visit to Nancy in France, Freud had witnessed certain somewhat impressive experiments by Bernheim and Liébeault, in the course of which patients, wakened from a condition of induced sleep and experiences of hallucination, had been pressed to recollect what had happened in their hypnotic state, and had been able to recall much of what had occurred or been felt.[5] This demonstrated that inaccessible mental material might be brought to the surface by other methods than recollection obtained in the course of hypnosis.

The Breuer-Freud investigations led to the publication of a joint paper under the title 'Preliminary Communication' in January

1 See Freud's obituary study of Charcot, written in 1893; *Complete Psychological Works of S. Freud,* Vol. III, pp. 11-23.

2 Ibid., pp. 18-22, for Freud's account of Charcot's methods.

3 Although in *Studies on Hysteria* (1895), English translation by James and Alix Strachey, London 1956, p. 260, Freud said: 'I had come fresh from the school of Charcot, and I regarded the linking of hysteria with the topic of sexuality as a sort of insult—just as the women patients themselves do'.

4 See Leon Chertok, 'Freud in Paris: A Crucial Stage', *International Journal of Psycho-Analysis,* Vol. 51 (1970), pp. 511-20.

5 This visit is referred to by Freud in his study 'On the History of the Psycho-Analytic Movement', *Complete Psychological Works of S. Freud,* Vol. XIV, p. 9, and in the *Complete Introductory Lectures on Psycho-analysis,* London 1971, p. 103.

1893.[6] This was favourably commented upon, and was followed by the appearance in 1895 of their joint work, *Studies on Hysteria,* regarded as marking a milestone in the history of significant psycho-analytic literature. The book still reflected the view that hypnosis was primarily necessary to enable patients to recollect emotional events, and to facilitate the discharge of pathogenic tensions.

The paths of Freud and Breuer then came to diverge. Various explanations have been offered for this. For one thing, they differed in their views concerning the extent to which sexuality played a role, by virtue of repression, in all cases. Breuer, though, had expressly stated that the sexual instinct was the most powerful source of neuroses.[7] Also Breuer did not apparently share the full measure of genuine enthusiasm felt by Freud for the possibilities opened by the theories and hypotheses formulated in *Studies on Hysteria.* In addition, Freud decided to dispense with hypnosis, which he found a difficult tool to use with many patients, and which he also felt could not provide a lasting recovery from symptoms. He wished to reach deeper into the sources of the wider conflicts affecting the personality.

This led Freud to the procedure of free association of thoughts, with the patient lying relaxed upon a couch. This enabled a thorough scientific investigation of psychic material, and facilitated insight into the character of the unconscious conflicts, and the patients' resistances to recovery. Gradually, with more and more refinements, a technique of treatment was developed, tending to approximate to the therapeutic process currently employed, with the physician acting for the most part as a tolerant, passive listener. He was also an interpreter where necessary.

In 1896 Freud first used the term 'psycho-analysis', although curiously enough, in relation to Breuer's method and not in respect to the technique that he was developing himself.[8]

6 Published in two separate parts in the issues of 1 and 15 January 1893 of the Berlin *Neurologisches Centralblatt.*

7 See *Studies on Hysteria* (English translation by James and Alix Strachey), London 1956, p. 200.

8 The actual passage is to be found in his paper of 1896, 'Heredity and the Aetiology of the Neuroses', and reads: 'I owe my results to a new method of psycho-analysis, Josef Breuer's exploratory procedure; it is a little intricate, but it is *irreplaceable,* so fertile has it shown itself to be in throwing light upon the obscure paths of unconscious ideation', *Complete Psychological Works of S. Freud,* Vol. III, p. 151. The word 'irreplaceable' should be noted, in the light of the new technique developed by Freud after ceasing collaboration with Breuer.

In 1897, Freud commenced a procedure of self-analysis, the fruits of which were represented by improvements in his psycho-analytic methodology, and by valuable insights into the unconscious factors governing the content of dreams.[9]

From 1895 onwards, Freud produced a number of seminal studies, papers, and books in which many of the fundamentals of psycho-analytic doctrine were first formulated. These contributions included his three classical works, *The Interpretation of Dreams* (1900), *The Psychopathology of Everyday Life* (1901), and *Three Contributions to the Theory of Sexuality* (1905). *The Psychopathology of Everyday Life,* dealing with the unconscious causes of slips of the tongue and pen, lapses of memory, mis-readings, and other parapraxes, had been preceded by an earlier paper on the same topic, and published in 1898 titled 'The Psychical Mechanism of Forgetfulness'.[10]

In 1903, the Vienna Psycho-Analytical Circle was founded, providing proof that, general hostility towards the theories of psycho-analysis notwithstanding, Freud had been able to attract followers and collaborators. In 1908 the first International Psycho-Analytical Congress was held at Salzburg, while in the following year Freud gave five lectures on the origins and development of psycho-analysis in the United States at Clark University, Massachusetts. Psycho-analysis had therefore taken root, and the end of this first period in its history can be taken as marked by the formal foundation of the International Psycho-Analytical Association in 1910. This was to lead to systematized training in the techniques of psycho-analysis.

While Freud was the central figure in the development of psycho-analytic theory and therapy, there were others of the first rank who made important contributions, and who, in several areas, both influenced Freud in his work and aided in consolidating his achievements. Among these were such men as Karl Abraham, who, among other contributions, dealt with the problems of libido development, symbolism, obsessional neurosis, and character formation; Ferenczi, who assisted in refining psycho-analytic therapy, did much to round off Freud's theoretical work, and is said to have foreshadowed psycho-analytic ego psychology; Ernest Jones, the biographer of Freud, who produced original studies in regard to symbolism, symbol formation, sublimation, and the basis of neuro-

[9] See W. W. Meissner, 'Freud's Methodology', *Journal of the American Psychoanalytic Association,* Vol. 19 (1971), p. 265, at p. 305.

[10] *Complete Psychological Works of S. Freud,* Vol. III, pp. 289-97.

tic symptoms; and Hanns Sachs who, among other things, contributed to the theory of dream interpretation and of perversions. Freud's colleagues or associates in this period also included Rank, Jung and Adler, who were later to diverge from the movement.

(2) Period 1910-1939

This period was marked, primarily, by the astonishing continued intellectual creativity of Freud, with the assistance of his followers, in the development of psycho-analytic doctrine. It terminated with his death, shortly after the outbreak of the Second World War, in September 1939.

Before dealing with the major additions made by Freud to psycho-analytic doctrine, the following points may be mentioned: (a) the psycho-analytic movement continued to spread, with ramifications in numerous countries, and this notwithstanding the separation from the movement of two notable associates, Adler and Jung in 1911 and 1913 respectively and notwithstanding also the effect of the First World War, 1914-1918; (b) psycho-analysis became strengthened by the efforts of many dedicated men to maintain its links with general medicine and psychiatry; (c) refinements were made in the techniques of therapy by a great number of practising analysts; (d) there was a substantial increase in psycho-analytic literature, including books and studies intended for the general public, and having the desired effect of removing much uninformed prejudice; (e) the systematic training of persons for the practice of psycho-analysis continued upon a more extensive scale; (f) more and more persons sought psycho-analytic treatment; and (g) child analysis came into being, and great strides were made in its development.

It is worth mentioning that in July 1926 the Council of the British Medical Association set up a Special Committee to investigate and report upon the subject of psycho-analysis. After meetings extending from March 1927 to May 1929, the Committee presented its Report in July 1929. In the 'Conclusions' to the Report, the Committee, after acknowledging that Freud had first used the term 'psycho-analysis', affirmed 'that in any scientific inquiry into the matter the claims of Freud and his followers to the use and definition of the term are just and must be respected'. However, in the body of the Report, after mentioning Freud's conclusions regarding the unconscious, repression, the existence of infantile sexuality, and the Oedipus complex, it described these conclusions of Freud as being 'of an extremely astonishing nature' and declared it 'not surprising that there has been a general incredulity towards Freud's methods and conclusions, so much so that some are unable to think that there could be sufficient evidence to establish them'.[11] The Report therefore evidences the resistance of medical opinion of about forty years ago to psycho-analysis, while it serves also to measure the degree of recognition accorded to the psycho-analytic movement at that time.

The major additions and clarifications made by Freud during this period included the following.

(i) The structural theory of personality as constituted by the ego, the id, and the super-ego, expounded in detail in *The Ego and the Id* (1923).

(ii) The modified theory of anxiety, and the clarification of the nature of neurosis, of symptoms, and inhibitions, as set out in his book, *Inhibitions, Symptoms and Anxiety* (1926).

(iii) The explanation of collective psychopathology contained in *Group Psychology and the Analysis of the Ego* (1921).

(iv) The concept of narcissism, and the theory regarding its place in the development of object-choice, as first outlined in the study, *On Narcissism: An Introduction* (1914), and the refinements added in later editions of his *Three Contributions to the Theory of Sexuality.*

(v) The concept of repetition-compulsion, which may be found referred to in *Beyond the Pleasure Principle* (1920).

(vi) The concept of the death instinct, and the theory regarding its relationship to sadism and masochism. The evolution of this concept in Freud's mind may be traced through three contributions among others—*Beyond the Pleasure Principle* (1920), *Civilization and its Discontents* (1930), and in the exchange of open letters with Albert Einstein in 1932.[12]

(vii) The revival by him of the concept of 'defence' to designate a technique which the ego may employ to cope with an inner conflict that may otherwise give rise to a neurosis. This was expounded to some extent in his book, *Inhibitions, Symptoms and Anxiety* (1926). Subsequently, the subject of the defence mechanisms of the ego was discussed in detail by his daughter, Anna Freud, in her standard work, *The Ego and the Mechanisms*

[11] Report, pp. 22, 9.

[12] His theory of the division of the basic instincts into Eros and the death instinct will be found set out in his work of 1939, *An Outline of Psycho-Analysis.*

of Defence (1936). In 1937 Dr Heinz Hartmann stressed the adaptive functions of the ego in that connection.

Again, as in the period 1882-1910, it would be wrong to disregard the contributions made by many other members of the psycho-analytic movement, which helped to consolidate the mainstream of the doctrine of psycho-analysis, while also confirming or adding to the results achieved by Freud.

(3) Period from 1939 to the present date

Initially, this period brought disaster and disruption to psycho-analysis in Europe, with the closing-down of psycho-analytic centres in occupied territory, coupled with the death or emigration of many skilled analysts. However, outside Europe, and in particular in the United States, psycho-analysis continued to maintain vitality and in some instances to show evidence of marked growth.

Europe has now largely recovered from this heavy blow, although in some cases reinstatement to pre-war standing has not proved possible. The recovery was well reflected in 1965 in the participation of European analysts in the 24th International Psycho-Analytical Congress held at Amsterdam. This Congress was of interest besides as an expression of the determination of psycho-analysts to strengthen psycho-analytical organization throughout the world at the branch and regional levels.

Since Amsterdam there have been three further International Psycho-Analytical Congresses, at Copenhagen in 1967, Rome in 1969, and Vienna in 1971. The extent of the participation in these gatherings, and the high level of the papers presented or delivered by participants can reasonably be taken as reflecting an increased vigour in the psycho-analytic movement.

Throughout the period, there has been a continuous trend of the making of major, valuable additions to psycho-analytic doctrine. Among these significant contributions have been: (a) Progress in depth in the domain of the theory and practice of child analysis,[13] with emphasis upon the investigation of such areas as the developmental needs of young children,[14] in relation to the influence of the

[13] See Anna Freud, 'A Short History of Child Analysis', *Psychoanalytic Study of the Child,* Vol. XXI (1966), pp. 7-14.

[14] See Anna Freud, *Normality and Pathology in Childhood. Assessments of Development,* London 1966, and her article, 'Indications and Contra-indications of Child Analysis', *Psychoanalytic Study of the Child,* Vol. XXIII (1968), pp. 37-46.

mother, and to the impact of environmental factors. In particular, important insights have been derived from the data of direct child observation, developed on a considerable scale. (b) Systematic development of the principles of psycho-analytic ego psychology, leading to greatly increased knowledge of the defence mechanisms of the ego. (c) Clarification of the nature of sublimation and neutralisation in relation to the instinctual drives, including aggressivity. (d) Continued efforts to improve the methodology of psycho-analysis. (e) Closer examination and elucidation of the theory of narcissism. (f) The investigation of values in relation to psycho-analysis. (g) The greater extension of psycho-analytic doctrine to cover questions of the relationship between personality and the environment, including the social environment.[15] This involves attention being given to both the quality and magnitude of man's environmental needs, particularly in respect to personality development. (h) Examination of the concept of the self, as distinct from the ego.[16] (i) The more general adoption by psycho-analysts of the approach that psycho-analytic doctrine should concern itself with the study of normality as well as that of abnormality. Thus, conflict itself may be of a normal nature, and not necessarily a characteristic of mental disorder or neurosis.

It is not to be doubted that currently psycho-analysis is holding its ground, and if the increase in membership—a ten-fold increase and more in some cases—of some branches of the International Psycho-Analytical Association since the pre-war years be a criterion in this connection, is growing in strength. As a method of scientific inquiry into unconscious mental phenomena and as a body of knowledge concerned with the central nature of personality it has yet to be displaced, in the absence of those far-reaching advances in neurology and neurochemistry which, as Freud foresaw, might create a body of doctrine into which the concepts and hypotheses of psycho-analysis could be absorbed. Its relevance to modern psychiatry is recognised, and is reflected in the training of many non-analytical psychiatrists in standard analytical techniques.

There is certainly evidence of a current revival of interest in

[15] Cf. Dr Heinz Hartmann in Sidney Hook (ed.), *Psychoanalysis . . .* , p. 14.

[16] See D. C. Levin, 'The Self: A Contribution to its Place in Theory and Technique', *International Journal of Psycho-Analysis,* Vol. 50 (1969), pp. 41-51.

psycho-analysis. According to one writer,[17] this springs from a 'widespread wish for a more systematic and cultural understanding of conflict in its normal and abnormal forms', and inasmuch as any family may have a member who is a drug addict, and therefore conventional good manners no longer compels us to pretend that only certain wayward groups contain members who are alcoholics, perverts, and so on, 'psychoanalysis has become interesting again both to the thinking public and to psychiatrists'.

[17] The author of a review of Dr D. W. Winnicott, *Playing and Reality,* and *Therapeutic Consultations in Child Psychiatry,* in the *Times Literary Supplement,* 17 December 1971, pp. 1579-80.

Appendix II

GLOSSARY OF PSYCHO-ANALYTICAL TERMS

This glossary is not intended to be exhaustive, but to cover some of the more frequently used expressions. Broad definitions are given rather than comprehensive explanations.

Abreaction: The 'working through' process, as a result of which the tension connected with a repressed wish, impulse, or urge is released by a patient through the course of free associations in which he reproduces and relives his memories and emotions, or expresses his thoughts in relation to the matter.

Acting out: Behaviour by way of response to a current situation, consisting of reacting in the same way as if this were the original situation giving rise to an instinctual urge, and enabling partial gratification of that urge.

Actual neurosis: Freud's expression for a nervous condition depending mainly on a somatic factor in sexual life, and the principal feature of which is the piling up of sexual excitement not adequately released.

Affect: A feeling or subjective sensation, painful or pleasurable, generally related to the working of the instincts.

Agoraphobia: A neurotic condition, involving an uncontrollable fear of open spaces, leading to avoidance of these, in order not to experience anxiety.

Ambivalence: A condition of coexistence of opposite feelings, generally of love and hate directed in regard to the same person as the object of these antithetic emotions.

Anaclitic type: A category of person who chooses as his first sexual object that same person upon whom he was dependent emotionally or for non-sexual needs; i.e., usually, under psycho-analytic doctrine, the mother or a mother-figure.

Anality: A condition stemming usually from an infantile fixation on the anal functions, and as a result of which an adult is over-concerned about such matters as meticulously regular and complete bowel elimination, and about general cleanliness, tidiness, and order. Anal characteristics are said to include conscientiousness, avariciousness, and stubbornness.

Anal stage: That stage in the pre-genital period of infantile sexual development when the child obtains pleasure from an interest in the anal zone.

Analytical rule: The rule that a patient undergoing psycho-analytic treatment must disclose or state in his free associations all that enters his mind during the analytical session, without deliberately refraining from revealing particular thoughts of which he is ashamed, or which he feels unwilling to make known to the analyst.

Anti-cathexis: This occurs when a resistance to a repressed feeling is manifested in the ego by an attitude opposite to that feeling. For example, a resistance to repressed hate of a person, who is also loved, may be expressed by an anti-cathexis of over-tenderness (see also *Cathexis*).

Anxiety (*neurotic*): An emotional condition involving uncontrollable fear and apprehension, irrespective of real danger, and generally manifested in physical as well as mental symptoms.

Anxiety hysteria: A phobic condition, in many instances, in which there is an attempt at flight from, or avoidance of the threatened condition of neurotic anxiety.

Anxiety neurosis: A neurosis in which the recurrence of anxiety states constitutes the predominant symptom.

Auto-erotism: A tendency to obtain sensual satisfaction from the parts of one's own body as the sexual object. Also represents an early stage of infantile development, before the transition to the narcissistic stage when the libido is directed to the self.

Castration complex: A group of attitudes, tendencies, and ideas having their common origin in an unconscious fear, arising in childhood, of loss of, or injury to the penis. In women, this same complex is said to be governed by infantile fantasies of earlier possession of the phallus, and of its loss through castration.

Catharsis: The 'cleansing' effect felt by the personality when by the free associations of repugnant or repulsive thoughts and ideas, the tension or uneasiness associated with such thoughts and ideas is discharged or released.

Cathexis: The investment of psychic energy, libidinal or aggressive, on some object, person, or idea, or as in the case of narcissism, even on the ego itself.

Compensation: A process by which a person affects an exaggerated attitude or posture by way of covering up some inferiority, state of insecurity, or other hidden mental condition.

Complex: A group of attitudes and tendencies of a person, linked together because of a common unconscious origin, and having a common emotional character.

Condensation: The mental process of fusion of a number of ideas, memories, fantasies, and attitudes into one, especially in the imagery of dreams.

Conscience: An expression for the totality of a person's internal moral standards, norms of behaviour, and levels of aspiration. The functions of a conscience are discharged by the super-ego.

Conversion: The process by which some repressed erotic or aggressive urge becomes transformed into physical or other overt symptom; cf. the expression 'conversion hysteria'.

Counter-cathexis: The application of psychic energy to the prevention of some instinctual urge, which has been warded off by repression or by a defence mechanism, from regaining its force or returning to consciousness.

Counter-transference: The emotional attitude of the analyst towards the patient, either by specific response to the patient's own transference relationship in regard to him, or as a matter of general reaction to the patient in the course of treatment.

Death instinct: The destructive instinct postulated by Freud as being present in every living being, 'striving to work its ruin and reduce life to its primal state of inert matter'.

Defence mechanisms of the ego: Processes or techniques availed of by the ego in order to protect itself from the inner dangers of the instinctual urges.

Defusion: The reverse of the so-called 'fusion' of the erotic and aggressive instincts; e.g. sadism in its complete form represents a blending of aggression and erotic delight in the sufferings of others, and the result of defusion is that the erotic element becomes disengaged.

Displacement: The transference of an emotional attitude from one person or object or idea to another usually similar person, object, or idea.

Ego: The largely conscious part of the mind, concerned with perception, rational thought and conduct, and adjustment to reality, and which is in a sense oriented to the self-preservation of the person.

Ego-ideal: An expression for the totality of ideals, norms, standards of conduct, and levels of aspiration set up as a mental image by which the person concerned measures the value of his ego and of his behaviour. It is sometimes treated as being synonymous with the super-ego.

Ego-syntonic: An epithet descriptive of the compatibility with the ego of ideas or tendencies originating in the instincts.

Empathy: A feeling of compatibility with another person, in respect to that person's ideas and attitudes, such feeling being conditioned generally by the mental process of identification with such other person.

Epinosic gain: The secondary gain from the continuance of symptoms, corresponding to some outside personal advantage or pleasure.

Erotogenic zones: The sensually responsive areas of the body.

Exhibitionism: A component tendency of sexuality, represented by the sensual feeling or pleasure obtained from the exhibition of the person, or the qualities or talents of the person. In the narrow sense, it can denote exhibition of the genitals.

Fixation: An early emotional attachment to some tendency, feeling, part of the body, or idea, and which has usually occurred in infancy, but has remained stationary without further progress or adjustment in the direction of a more mature phase of development.

Free associations: The free expression or revelation of thoughts, ideas, and feelings as they enter a person's mind in the course of psycho-analytic treatment. See also *Analytical rule*.

Frustration: In the strict sense, the blocking by external reality of the satisfaction of an instinctual urge. The term has also been used to denote the counteraction of an instinctual urge by some opposing force within the psyche.

Id: That unconscious part of the mind, which provides a storehouse for the basic instinctive urges and drives of personality, being those demanding immediate gratification or satisfaction, irrespective of rational considerations.

Identification: The mental process by which one person comes to feel in the same way as another person, being often a person to whom he looks up or whom he idealizes, with the result that, so to speak, he becomes at one with that person. There can also be identification with an introjected personality. See also *Introjection.*

Identity, sense of: Broadly speaking, a feeling of awareness of the self, coupled with some reliance upon the fact that this same self has much the same meaning for other persons, or for other members of a group to which the subject belongs.

Introjection: The process, somewhat akin to identification, of the inner acceptance or taking over of the characteristics and attitudes of another person, generally by way of a standard of future behaviour.

Latency period: The period of relative dormancy of sexuality in children, commencing as from the end of infantile sexual development in the fifth or sixth year, and terminating in or after the pre-puberty phase in the eleventh, twelfth, or thirteenth year, whereupon there is a renaissance of sexuality.

Libido: The psychic energy behind the sexual drive.

Malaise: A vague feeling, generally speaking, of lack of perspective in life, or of disillusionment and absence of contentment, or of inability to detect any sense or significance in living. It should be distinguished from a neurosis.

Masochism: A tendency of an aggressive character, directed inwards against the self, so that the self experiences either physical or mental pain, accompanied with some gratification of sensuality from the suffering.

Megalomania: An overvaluation of the self, primarily due, so it is claimed, to a pathological or almost pathological intensification of narcissism.

Melancholia: A morbid mental disorder, with symptoms in general of acute depression, which symptoms are, insofar as the condition is one of psychological origin, attributed to the operation of an excessively severe super-ego.

Narcissism: The attitude of a person whose libidinal energy is self-invested, at the expense of being directed to an object other than the self.

Neurosis: A disturbance of the personality, with symptoms of anxiety or suffering, or of morbid inhibitions of the ego, such symptoms being usually the outcome of a conflict between repressed wishes or tendencies, and the forces opposing gratification.

Neutralization: A generalized term applied by some psychoanalysts to the process of countering or rendering innocuous the instinctual urges, more often applied however in relation to the aggressive urge. There may be some overlapping with sublimation, q.v.

Nosogenesis: The classification of a neurotic condition or mental disorder according to the circumstances and the nature of its onset, or of its initial cause.

Object: That to which a libidinal aggressive urge is directed, or which is invested with libidinal or aggressive energy.

Objective anxiety: Anxiety representing a reaction of fear and apprehension when confronted with a real danger. As Freud put it: 'Objective danger is a danger that is known, and objective anxiety is anxiety about a known danger of this sort'.

Obsessional neurosis: A neurosis in which the general symptoms are compulsive ideas, acts, or tendencies, not dictated by rational considerations, together, usually, with a feeling of anxiety if the ritual-like acts are not performed.

Oedipus complex: A group of tendencies, ideas, and feelings constituted in infancy, in the case of boys, by love of the mother and an accompanying antagonism towards the father, but which under a supposed threat of castration may become repressed, leaving generally as a heritage a severe super-ego, continuing into adulthood. In the case of girls, there is a corresponding complex, sometimes known as the 'Electra' complex, involving an attitude of rivalry towards the mother and love of the father, but because there is no similar fear of a future castration, this complex is not submerged under repression, and may continue for some indefinite time, without the formation of a stern super-ego.

Omnipotence of thought: The notion that a mere wish or mental process has magical value or force, in that it will produce a contemplated event or consequence. Because of his disdain for 'omnipotence of thought', Freud was critical of letters to him, conveying good wishes for the future.

Over-determination of a symptom: A multiplicity of factors, operating to produce a symptom, where normally one factor or governing cause would be sufficient for this purpose.

Paranoia: A mental disorder, characterized generally by feelings of being persecuted. These feelings are claimed to be symptomatic of an inner reaction against unconscious homosexual wishes or fears.

Paranosic gain: The primary gain from a symptom or symptoms; e.g., corresponding to the satisfaction obtained therefrom, or to the fact that the symptom may serve to relieve a person of a burden of guilt.

Paraphenia: A general term, apparently first coined by Freud, and embracing paranoia and schizophrenia.

Parapraxes: A compendious expression for slips of the tongue, misreadings, errors in writing or typewriting, lapses of memory, and symptomatic acts, ultimately due, according to Freud, to the operation of unconscious psychic processes.

Phobia: A neurosis consisting in the avoidance of, or aversion to certain places, things, animals, etc., without rational justification, and so as not to experience uncontrollable or almost uncontrollable anxiety.

Pleasure principle: This describes the governing aim or purpose of the impulses in the id, namely, to seek immediate gratification, irrespective of the consequences rationally considered.

Polarities: Antithetic mental phenomena or tendencies which may happen to be blended in the personality; e.g., pleasure-pain, masculine-feminine, and active-passive.

Preconscious: That part of the unconscious which functions more or less as conscious activities do, and which may readily become conscious without having to overcome resistances or repression.

Primary process: The earlier, more primitive mechanism of operation of the mind, which finds expression in dreams, and the principal feature of which is the tendency towards a complete discharge of psychic energy without delay.

Projection: The psychological process of attribution to another person of an attitude, wish, or tendency, especially where this is felt to be repugnant to oneself; e.g., the projection of guilt, as where one person who feels some guilt over the commission of a mistake will project that feeling to another, so as to make that other person responsible for the mistake.

Psychosis: A pathological condition, characterised primarily by basic disturbance of the personality, and by loss of reality. According to Freud, the distinction between a neurosis and a psychosis is that in the case of a neurotic person the ego continues to be dependent upon reality, notwithstanding that the id is injuriously affected, whereas in the case of a psychotic person, the ego will in the service of the id withdraw from reality.

Rationalization: A defence mechanism of the ego, whereby a feeling of guilt or other unacceptable attitude of the self in relation to one's conduct, is negated by some form of reasoning in justification of that conduct which, though superficially cogent from the standpoint of the ego, is in substance fallacious.

Reaction formation: A defence mechanism of the ego against an unacceptable or repugnant tendency, manifested by an excessive reaction of the personality in the opposite direction; e.g., a posture of aggressive arrogance as a reaction formation to a feeling of insecurity arising from repressed instinctual impulses.

Reality principle: This describes the aim or purpose of the ego to forego, in a rational manner, an immediate pleasure and/or experience pain for the purpose of a more satisfactory end-result, in which eventually pain may be minimized, and pleasure maximized.

Regression: The return, psychically speaking, to an earlier, usually infantile phase of a person's psychological or sexual development, or to an earlier fixation.

Rejection: (1) The thrusting away of an urge or impulse which is condemned by the judgment of the ego. (2) The feeling in infancy that parents have withdrawn their love (this may be re-animated in adulthood as an irrational feeling of being rejected by society).

Repetition-compulsion: The tendency of the personality, conditioned by the instincts, to continue repeating certain earlier characteristics or attitudes of emotive significance, usually those developed or experienced in infancy, and which have been the object of repression. This repetition may occur either in the conscious life or in dreams.

Repression: The process of rejecting and excluding from consciousness certain unacceptable or unwelcome instinctual impulses, memories, wishes, and fantasies, mainly related to early childhood.

Resistance: The opposition, most generally unconscious, of the patient in analysis, either to becoming aware of unconscious tendencies, wishes, or attitudes, or generally to recovery from the condition for which he is being treated. Five forms of resistance have been identified: (1) repression-resistance; (2) transference resistance; (3) resistance flowing from the secondary gain involved in the illness; (4) resistance due to the unconscious need for punishment, the illness representing the punishment; and (5) repetition-compulsion resistance.

Sadism: A tendency of an aggressive character, directed outwards against others, for the purpose of inflicting pain, or involving satisfaction from the fact that pain has been inflicted. Sadism is characterized by the accompanying sensuality.

Sado-masochism: A tendency constituted by a blending of sadism and masochism, q.v.

Schizophrenia: A psychosis, which may take a number of forms, and which is characterised primarily by a strong tendency to retreat from reality, acute emotional instability, and thought disturbances.

Secondary process: The mechanism of operation of the mind, consisting of delaying, modifying, or controlling the discharge of mental energy, and governed by the conscious, rational control of the ego.

Sensate ego: The ego regarded not only as a problem-solving agency, but as the centre of sensations and personal feelings.

Sublimation: The channelling of the instinctual drives in directions other than their primal aims, and enabling those drives to find gratification to some extent in fulfilling certain non-instinctual aims.

Super-ego: That division of the mind, described by Anna Freud as an 'inner court of judgment', inasmuch as it represents an internal incorporation of the authority of parents and parent-figures, constituting the source of inner moral dictates and prohibitions, as well as of standards and ideals established internally. It may be treated as discharging the functions of a conscience.

Transference: The emotional relationship which develops on the part of a patient towards his analyst after some progress has been made beyond the early phases of the analysis, and which represents largely a re-animation of infantile attitudes and emotions. The interpretation of the transference relationship is one of the cornerstones of psycho-analytic therapy.

Trauma: Broadly speaking, an emotional shock, as the result of injuries or other painful event, and which has a disturbing effect on the personality, either temporary or permanent.

Undoing: A defence mechanism of the ego, whereby an experience of a painful character is in effect treated as if it had never occurred.

Wish fulfilment: The gratification of a wish, conscious or unconscious, either in dreams or in symptoms. The wish need not represent a rationally felt desire of the person concerned.

Appendix III

MODERN DEVELOPMENTS IN PSYCHIATRY AND THE LAW[1]

In the last hundred years, modern psychiatry has developed to an extent that is almost inconceivable by comparison with the stage it had attained in the mid-nineteenth century. In theory, methodology, and therapy it is entirely a modern medical science. Psychoanalysis itself, which contributed so much to the progress made in psychiatry during the present century, is a product only of the last ninety years. Yet the courts continue to be governed by leading decisions on testamentary capacity and on legal responsibility, including criminal responsibility, which were given before modern psychiatry had even begun to evolve.

It is only to be expected that modern psychiatry would outpace the law, and in fact has outpaced it. The result is a strange contradiction between the assumptions on which leading judicial authorities on insanity are based, and the established foundations of modern psychiatry. Leading judges and jurists, on the one hand, and eminent psychiatrists, on the other, have drawn attention to this contradiction and to the urgent necessity of removing it. Thus the late Mr Justice Cardozo of the United States Supreme Court, commenting upon the defence of insanity to a criminal charge, said:

> Everyone concedes that the present definition of insanity has little relation to the truths of mental life. . . . Conceivably the twilight zone between sanity and insanity is so broad and so vague as to bid defiance to exact description. . . . If insanity is not to be a defence, let us say so frankly and even brutally,

[1] Reprinted, with some slight revisions, from *Australian Law Journal*, Vol. 16, p. 227.

> but let us not mock ourselves with a definition that patters with reality. Such a method is neither good morals, nor good science, nor good law.[2]

A leading English psychiatrist, commenting upon the obsolescence of the concepts of 'a partial delusion' and 'monomania' declared:

> The doctrine of partial delusion or monomania has been abandoned—not because of a change in fashion but because of an accumulation of facts. It is essential that the law should take cognisance of facts, which in science are always unfolding and developing, whereas the accretions which constitute legal tradition tend all the other way, crystallising and stereotyping a limited set of rules and definitions which have been laid down in the past.[3]

A distinguished American psychiatrist, also commented upon the necessity for the medical and legal professions finding some common ground in the administration of the law with respect to mentally unsound persons:

> Although the lawyer and the psychiatrist speak a different language and follow widely variant methodologies, there are points of contact in every day necessities where they should learn their mutual languages and become aware of the variant methods of arriving at pragmatic solutions of simple or intricate social misbehaviour.[4]

There is little doubt that both professions, to some degree anyway, realise the necessity for change. The difficulty lies in cementing the two points of view. Perhaps the psychiatrist is too unduly impatient with the lawyer who fails to appreciate psychological truths which are not too easy to grasp. On his side, the lawyer does not look for criticism from the psychiatrist, but for constructive suggestion which will bring the administration of the law into accord with the conclusions of medical science. If satisfactory legal rules are to be worked out, it is imperative that the lawyer and the psychiatrist should each seek to understand what is in the other's mind.

Insanity or mental unsoundness, broadly speaking, impinges on the law in two fields: the field of capacity; and that of responsibility. Another area in which psychiatric conditions may play some role, is that of accident liability and compensation, where one ingredient of the claim for damages is, for example, a supervening neurosis of the accident victim.

2 *Bulletin of New York Academy of Medicine,* Vol. 5, (1929), p. 581.

3 R. D. Gillespie in Journal of Comparative Legislation and International Law, Vol. XVI, p. 322.

4 Dr Smith Ely Jelliffe, Current Legal Thought, Vol. II, 1935-36, p. viii.

In principle, the rules of law governing the capacity or responsibility of mentally affected individuals, or determining the measure of compensation for a supervening psychiatric disorder, ought to depend upon exact psychiatric knowledge. It is the burden of criticisms such as that of the late Mr Justice Cardozo cited above, that the rules turn not so much upon exact psychiatric truths, as upon assumptions concerning human personality, antedating the development of modern psychiatry.

Technically, there are two stages in the process as it comes before the court: establishing that some condition of mental disorder does exist; and proof that this condition, once established to exist, is of such a degree or kind as to satisfy the legal tests of incapacity or irresponsibility. The general criticism is that at both stages the law is not consistent with the teachings of modern psychiatry. It is claimed that the law is still based upon elementary psychological concepts in which, as a rough test, recognition is given only to the most marked types of psychiatric disorders as justifying findings of incapacity or irresponsibility.

It is important first to consider in what way modern psychiatry, influenced by the teachings of psycho-analysis, has developed from the primitive theory and methodology of the mid-nineteenth century. It would be fair to say that one hundred years ago any kind of psychiatric disorder was regarded as an abnormality putting the individual suffering from it in a class distinct from that of ordinary human beings, that is to say, constituted him an insane person. In particular, if a person suffered from a single delusion, that delusion was regarded in the light of a disease afflicting the personality, but not as being an expression of the whole personality. Emphasis was laid on the cognitive aspects of the mentally unsound personality. Did the person concerned know or understand certain things which were clear to ordinary people? Finally, the classifications of mental and nervous disorders were extraordinarily primitive when judged in relation to the present day elaborate and refined classifications.

The teachings of modern psychiatry and psycho-analysis are entirely different. The mentally unsound individual is treated as differing in degree only from normal persons. Normal persons are considered as possessing incipiently all those tendencies which when aggravated or exposed to particular circumstances may produce psychiatric disorders. Every person therefore is inherently a potentially mentally unsound individual. It follows that the terms 'sanity' and 'insanity' in the medical vocabulary today are to some extent meaningless from the standpoint of psychiatry. Emphasis is laid upon the unity of the personality as a whole. A psychiatrist would treat a delusion not as a separate disease malignly afflicting the personality, but as a symptom of the entire personality considered in relation to it. Whereas formerly the morbid cognitive aspects of the mentally unsound personality were stressed, today greater emphasis is laid on the emotional side. It is realised that the roots of the great majority of mental diseases affecting cognition or volition lie in the emotions, in the deeper unconscious or instinctive layers of the personality. Finally, it has been established that mental and nervous diseases are capable of almost infinite variety, although definite classifications are possible within that range. Modern psychiatry has been able to distinguish the neuroses from the psychoses, and to a certain extent the mental diseases of somatic origin from those of purely psychological origin. These distinctions are well recognised by medical science. Present-day classifications thus render the elementary typology of a century ago completely out of date.

Considered in relation to modern psychiatry, much of the traditional legal learning as to mentally unsound individuals, particularly the statements and rulings contained in certain binding judicial precedents, assumes the character rather of legal metaphysics than of forensic psychiatry.

By far the greatest criticism upon this ground has been directed against the law affecting the field of responsibility, and particularly criminal responsibility. The rulings in 1843 in *M'Naghten's Case*[5] in regard to defences, upon the ground of insanity, to a criminal charge have received the severest condemnation. The principal ruling in this case was as follows:—

> To establish a defence on the ground of insanity, it must be clearly proved that, at the time of committing the act, the party accused was labouring under such a defect of reason, from disease of the mind, as not to know the nature and quality of the act he was doing, or, if he did know it, that he did not know he was doing what was wrong.

Broadly then, the test is based upon the accused's knowledge of right or wrong. But it is too primitive to reflect the teachings of modern psychiatry. It appears to have been devised with the object of providing a criterion simple enough to be readily applied by a lay jury, and of confining irresponsibility to cases of extreme psychopathological conditions as these were understood in the early days of mental medicine. That, in the light of modern psychiatry,

[5] 10 Cl. and F. 200.

the psychological assumptions underlying the rulings are regarded as erroneous or objectionable upon grounds of logical inconsistency is indicated by the vast literature, predominantly of a critical nature, generated by the difficulties experienced in applying the rulings to concrete cases.[6]

Moreover, the *M'Naghten* test was rejected by the United States Court of Appeals for the District of Columbia in 1954 in the case of *Durham v. United States* in favour of a rule that if the crime be 'the product of mental disease or mental defect' at the time of commission, this causality being established beyond all reasonable doubt, the accused is not criminally responsible.[7]

One of the *M'Naghten* rulings related to the presence of a specific delusion. In this event, it was laid down that a defence of insanity by the accused was to be considered in the same category of responsibility as if the facts in respect of which the delusion existed were real. It would be a fair criticism by a modern psychiatrist of this ruling that it signifies that the law accepts the delusion, but requires the accused to reason about it as if he were sane.

In fact, the basic assumption that the cognitive faculties are the sole criterion of psychiatric health, and therefore of criminal responsibility, is false. Modern medical science has shown the great importance of the emotional and volitional factors in psychiatric disorders. Disturbances in the cognitive sphere may not be sufficiently marked to prevent the subject from having some conception of the difference between right and wrong, but the subject may be suffering from severe emotional disturbance affecting his conduct, as in the case of an irresistible impulse, or in the case of an unconscious need for punishment which compels him to commit a crime in order to suffer the penalty.

The *M'Naghten Case,* and other decisions on legal responsibility in the mid-nineteenth century, gave expression to the then pre-

6 The *M'Naghten* rulings were considered by the English Royal Commission on Capital Punishment in its Report of 1953 (Cmd. 8932), at pp. 75 *et. seq.* and 116; the Commission recommended their abrogation. A new rule regarding a defence to a murder charge on the ground of mental disorder was inserted in section 2 of the English Homicide Act 1957; see Chapter XIII. See also for discussion of the rulings: Howard, *Australian Criminal Law,* 2nd edn., 1970, pp. 327-41; Wootton, *Social Science and Social Pathology,* 1959, Chapter VIII, and article, 'Diminished Responsibility: A Layman's View', *Law Quarterly Review,* Vol. 76 (1960), pp. 224-39; and N. Walker, 'M'Naghten's Ghost', *The Listener,* 29 August 1963, p. 303.

7 214 F.2d 862; and cf. Morris, University of Western Australia *Annual Law Review,* Vol. 3 (1955), p. 309 for comment upon this decision.

vailing psychological notions that moral sentiments, the conception of right and wrong, were self-sufficient entities of the mind. They failed to recognise that diseases afflicting the emotional and volitional spheres of the mind might completely inhibit moral sentiments. Moreover, a delusion was treated as a disease in itself, instead of as an expression of some deeper psychological condition affecting the whole personality of the individual. Nor was it appreciated that a person suffering from a specific delusion might be able to reason otherwise in a perfectly rational manner, but certain conduct would nevertheless be the inevitable outcome of the condition of which the delusion was a symptom. This is a proposition of an almost commonplace nature for those familiar with the psycho-analytical literature concerned with compulsive obsessional disorders; many of those persons suffering from such disorders have been of the highest intellectual capacity.

The same erroneous assumptions as to mental disorder in relation to criminal responsibility coloured the traditional law in respect to testamentary incapacity. Consider the following passage from the judgment of Cockburn, C.J., in the leading case of *Banks v. Goodfellow,*[8] where he was dealing with the exercise of the testamentary power:

> It is essential to the exercise of such a power that the testator *shall understand* the nature of the act and its effect; *shall understand* the extent of the property of which he is disposing; *shall be able to comprehend and appreciate the claims to which he ought to give effect;* and, with a view to the latter object, that no disorder of the mind shall poison his affections, pervert his sense of right, or prevent the exercise of his natural faculties—that *no insane delusion shall influence his will* in disposing of his property and bring about a disposal of it which, if the mind had been sound, would not have been made. Here, then, we have the measure of the degree of mental power which should be insisted on. If the human instincts and affections, or the moral senses become perverted by mental disease; if insane suspicion, or aversion, take the place of natural affection; if reason and judgment are lost, *and the mind becomes a prey to insane delusions calculated to interfere with and disturb its functions,* and to lead to a testamentary disposition due only to their baneful influence —in such a case it is obvious that the condition of the testamentary power fails, and that a will made under such circumstances ought not to stand.

Here again the emphasis is laid unduly upon the cognitive functions

[8] (1870) L.R. 5 Q.B., at p. 565.

of the mind at the expense of the emotional and volitional aspects.

Further, it will be observed that, as in the *M'Naghten Case,* a delusion is treated as a category of disease affecting the personality, instead of as a symptom of some general condition of the psyche. Moreover, the judgment appears to neglect the case of a testator, who may be able to reason quite rationally about his estate and the claims of his relatives upon it, yet be afflicted by some morbid emotional disorder, not necessarily of a delusional character, which may militate against the just and proper use of his testamentary power. Although modern psychiatry is quite definite about the existence of such a type of morbid mental condition, there have been instances of the refusal by courts to recognise it.[9]

Apart from the areas of criminal responsibility and testamentary capacity, there has been a similar over-emphasis upon the cognitive faculties of the mind in the cases of socially deviant behaviour, such as homosexual criminal offences, vagrancy and prostitution. Psycho-analysts have been able to show what complicated unconscious or emotional factors condition the commission of such offences, and how little responsive the persons concerned are to any remedial influence on their cognitive or rational faculties. They have also demonstrated that it is impossible to treat each of these categories as expressive of one uniform psychological condition, although this has sometimes been the approach of certain judges. For example, each homosexual offender will be found to have an unconscious mental background, peculiar to himself and to the circumstances of the development of his psyche. Moreover, psycho-analytical experience has confirmed that optimistic expectations by courts or parole boards, of rehabilitation, or of emancipation from such conditions of deviant behaviour are to be discounted. A formidable amount of psycho-analytical treatment is often required even to modify these conditions, and in many cases the conditions remain completely intractable.

It may be convenient here to consider briefly other matters in which deficiencies appear by comparison with modern psychiatry. The legal terminology of mental unsoundness has been confused, and hopelessly out of touch with medical science, although there has recently been some improvement. Such traditional expressions as *'non compos mentis'*, 'lunatic', 'mania', 'monomania', 'partial insanity', 'defect of the reason', and 'disease of the mind', although gradually tending to disappear, nevertheless continue to creep into

[9] See, e.g., the English decision of *In the Estate of Bohrmann* (1938), 1 All E.R. 271, at p. 279.

the judgments of courts. It might be a useful reform if the word 'insanity' were completely dropped from the medico-legal vocabulary. According to Halsbury's *Laws of England* (2nd edition):

> The legal terminology of insanity is neither consistent nor comprehensive. The various expressions denoting insanity are not used in an uniform sense, nor are there any names to distinguish civil incapacity from criminal irresponsibility.[10]

There are indeed cogent reasons why the so-called presumption of sanity ought to be reconsidered.[11] Presumptions of law exist as a rule where there is a choice between two situations, of which one is by common accord the more usual. But there is no such definite choice between sanity and insanity. The variety of psychiatric disorders is infinite, and the term 'insanity' is quite inappropriate when used as of general application. Moreover, the presumption of sanity has sometimes been applied in the following circumstances: evidence of some psychiatric disorder has been put before the court, but although the evidence may have disclosed some morbid condition perfectly familiar to psychiatrists, the court has been reluctant to recognise any type of mental unsoundness save the most pronounced psychopathological condition, and has balanced against the evidence of mental disorder the so-called presumption of sanity. Such a method of proceeding on the evidence is unscientific and out of touch with realities.

One further respect in which the law is deficient is in its failure logically to work out the specific types of psychiatric disorder which will bring about either complete incapacity and irresponsibility, or some restricted capacity and restricted responsibility. Clearly, a psychiatric disorder affecting capacity may differ fundamentally from a morbid condition of the psyche affecting responsibility.

The reluctance of practising lawyers and judges to accept the now established conclusions of modern psychiatric science is no doubt due to experience of psychiatrists in the witness box. Under present conditions, expert evidence of the subject's mental condition is put before the court by the parties who are at issue. From its very nature, the partisan expert system lends itself to abuse and absurdity. Partisan experts, whether psychiatrists or other scientific witnesses, are notoriously biased. Lord Campbell's dictum in 1843, that scientific witnesses 'come with a bias on their minds to support the cause in which they are embarked',[12] is no less true today than it was then. As one writer in the *Harvard Law Review* put it:

[10] Vol. 21, p. 273.
[11] Ibid., Vol. 16, p. 205.
[12] *Tracy Peerage Case* (1843), 10 Cl. ane F. 154, at p. 191.

> Every litigation in which the question of mental condition is involved presents—if the litigants can afford the cost—the spectacle of two groups of equally distinguished psychiatrists testifying to mutually contradictory conclusions and each exercising a degree of ingenuity in advocacy of which a lawyer would be proud—or ashamed—in the effort to establish the consistency of the evidence with the thesis it conceives itself to have been paid to advocate.[13]

Under these circumstances, it is not to be wondered at that judges are insistent that the final responsibility of adjudicating on the psychiatric condition of the subject rests with the judge or jury. The court or jury is to form its own conclusions upon the testimony before it, part of which testimony is the evidence of psychiatrists (see *Richmond v. Richmond,* 111 L.T. 273). The fact remains, however, that the judge is not often equipped to grasp the subtleties of psychiatry, and properly to interpret the medical testimony. In the result, the procedure is doubly defective, and this double effect produces a vicious circle, with the judge ultimately obliged to make a choice between the two theses submitted to the court.

There are two possible methods by which the law can narrow the gap between it and the advances in modern psychiatry: (1) the judicial method, with the courts prepared to give effect to new developments, and adjust the legal principles correspondingly; and (2) the legislative method, that is to say by statutory changes incorporating the results of the progress in psychiatry.

In the case of the judicial method, what happens has been well put in one celebrated American case (namely, *State v Jones,* 50 N.H. 369):

> We have consented to receive those facts (of science) developed and ascertained by the researches and observations of our own day, instead of adhering blindly to dogmas which were accepted as facts of science and erroneously promulgated as principles of law fifty or one hundred years ago.

The use of this method depends largely upon the boldness of judges, and their breadth of mind in keeping pace with modern medical developments. Obviously, therefore, this method would not be satisfactory where fundamental reforms were required. There is a danger too that the judge might act on a mistaken view of mental disorder or psychiatric affliction which the mature and considered judgment of the majority of psychiatrists would have rejected.

Legislation thus appears to be the primary method whereby reforms of a basic character, enabling the law to keep abreast of

[13] Vol. 33, p. 881.

progress in modern psychiatry, are likely to be achieved. Judges would prefer to put the onus upon legislatures of giving effect to advances in psychiatry. Certainly it is true that, in the last two decades, much far-reaching legislation has been passed by Parliaments in the United Kingdom and in the Australian States in an endeavour to stay in line with new developments in psychiatry.[14]

Whether the judicial or the legislative method be employed, it is above all important that legal principles or legal formulations should be firmly based upon the truths revealed by advances in psychiatry. As a distinguished judge, Judge Manfred Lachs of the International Court of Justice, has said:

> Whenever law is confronted with facts of nature or technology, its solutions must rely on criteria derived from them. For law is intended to resolve problems posed by such facts and it is herein that the link between law and the realities of life is manifest. It is not legal theory which provides answers to such problems; all it does is to select and adapt the one which best serves its purposes and integrate it within the framework of law.[15]

[14] See, e.g., the English Mental Health Act, 1959, and the New South Wales Mental Health Act, 1958, as amended.

[15] In the decision of the Court in the *North Sea Continental Shelf Cases*, I.C.J. Reports, 1969, 3, p. 222.

BIBLIOGRAPHY[1]

Abraham, K., *Clinical Papers and Essays on Psychoanalysis,* ed. by Abraham, H. C., translated by Abraham, H. C., and Ellison, D. R., Hogarth Press, London 1955.

Alexander, F., *The Scope of Psychoanalysis, 1921-1961: Selected Papers,* Basic Books, New York 1961.

Alexander, F., Eisenstein, S., and Grotjahn, M., ed., *Psychoanalytic Pioneers,* Basic Books, New York 1966.

Anderson, John, *Studies in Empirical Philosophy,* Angus & Robertson, Sydney 1962.

Arnheim, R., *Towards a Psychology of Art: Collected Essays,* Faber & Faber, London 1967.

Bastide, R., *Sociologie et Psychanalyse,* Presses Universitaires de France, Paris 1950.

Braithwaite, R. B., *Scientific Explanation. A Study of the Function of Theory, Probability and Law in Science,* Cambridge University Press 1953.

Colby, K. M., *An Introduction to Psychoanalytic Research,* Basic Books, New York 1960.

Deutsch, H., *Psychoanalysis of the Neuroses,* translated by Robson-Scott, W. D., Hogarth Press, London 1951.

Einstein, A., and Freud, S., *Why War*? International Institute of Intellectual Cooperation, Paris 1933.

Erikson, E. H., *Childhood and Society,* 2nd edition, revised and enlarged, W. W. Norton, New York 1963.

[1] This is intended only as a short bibliography of selected books and studies.

Fairbairn, W. R. D., *Psychoanalytic Studies of the Personality,* Tavistock, London 1952.

Ferenczi, S., *Further Contributions to the Theory and Technique of Psychoanalysis,* Hogarth Press, London 1950.

Flugel, J. C., *A Hundred Years of Psychology, 1833-1933*, 3rd edition, 1964, with revision by West, D. J., Duckworth, London 1964.

————, *Man, Morals and Society. A Psycho-Analytical Study,* Peregrine edition, Penguin Books, Harmondsworth 1962.

Freud, A., *Introduction to Psycho-Analysis for Teachers. Four Lectures,* translated by Low, Barbara, Allen & Unwin, London 1931.

————, *The Ego and the Mechanisms of Defence,* International Universities Press, New York 1946.

Freud, S., *The Standard Edition of the Complete Psychological Works of Sigmund Freud,* translated under the general editorship of Strachey, J. in collaboration with Freud, A., Hogarth Press, London 1956-1966 (23 volumes).

Hartmann, H., *Essays on Ego Psychology: Selected Problems in Psychoanalytic Theory,* Hogarth Press, London 1964.

Hook, S., ed., *Psychoanalysis, Scientific Method and Philosophy,* Grove Press, New York 1959.

Jeffrey, H., *Scientific Inference,* 2nd edition. Cambridge University Press 1957.

Katz, J., Goldstein, J., and Dershowitz, A. M., *Psychoanalysis, Psychiatry and Law,* The Free Press, New York 1967.

Kubie, L. S., *Practical and Theoretical Aspects of Psychoanalysis,* International Universities Press, New York 1957.

Jones, E., *The Life and Work of Sigmund Freud,* Basic Books, New York 1953, 1955, and 1957 (3 volumes).

Lorand, A. S., *Technique of Psychoanalytic Therapy,* International Universities Press, New York 1961.

Misiak, H., and Sexton, Virginia, S., *History of Psychology. An Overview,* Grune & Stratton, New York 1966.

Ricoeur, P., *De l'Interprétation. Essai sur Freud,* Editions du Sueil, Paris 1966.

Rosenfeld, H. A., *Psychotic States: a Psychoanalytical Approach,* International Universities Press, New York 1965.

Salzman, L., *Developments in Psychoanalysis,* Grune & Stratton, New York 1962.

Strachey, A., *The Unconscious Motives of War: a Psychoanalytical Contribution,* Allen & Unwin, London 1957.

Waelder, R., *Basic Theory of Psychoanalysis,* International Universities Press, New York 1960.

———, *Psychoanalytic Avenues to Art,* Hogarth Press, London 1965.

———, *Psychological Aspects of War and Peace,* Geneva Studies, Vol X, No. 2, Geneva Research Centre, 1939.

Wollheim, R., *Freud,* Fontana/Collins, London 1971.

INDEX